PETER HØEG was born in 1957 and followed various callings – dancer, actor, fencer, sailor, mountaineer – before he turned seriously to writing. He published his first novel in 1988. That book was already, according to Søren Schou of *Information* magazine, evidence enough that Høeg was "the foremost storyteller of his generation". This was followed by his first short-story collection, then by *Miss Smilla's Feeling for Snow*, which became an immediate bestseller and received international acclaim.

BORDERLINERS

PETER HØEG

Translated from the Danish
by Barbara Haveland

THE HARVILL PRESS

First published in Denmark with the title
De måske egnede
by Munksgaard/Rosinante, Copenhagen 1993

First published in Great Britain, 1995
by The Harvill Press

2 4 6 8 9 7 5 3 1

A CIP catalogue record for this title
is available from the British Library

ISBN 1 86046 036 4 (hardback)
1 86046 037 2 (paperback)

Photoset in Linotron Sabon by
Rowland Phototypesetting Ltd, Bury St Edmunds, Suffolk

Printed and bound in Great Britain
by Hartnolls Limited, Bodmin, Cornwall

I

WHAT IS TIME?

We ascended towards the light, five floors up, and split up into thirteen rows facing the god who unlocks the gates of morning. Then there was a pause, then in came Biehl.

Why the pause?

When asked straight out about his pauses by one of the bright girls, Biehl had first gone absolutely still. Then he – who normally never referred to himself as "I" – then he had said, slowly and with great gravity, as though he were surprised by the question, and perhaps even by his own reply: "When I speak, you should listen, first and foremost, to my pauses. They speak louder than my words."

And so it was with the interval between the hall going absolutely still and him coming in and up to the podium. An eloquent pause. His own words.

The morning song was followed by a pause, the Lord's Prayer recited by Biehl, pause, a short hymn, pause, a traditional patriotic song, pause and finish, and he left the hall as he had come, briskly, almost running.

What feeling was there in the hall while this was going on?

There was no special feeling, really, I said, it was early in the morning and people were tired, and could we finish now, I was getting a headache, and it was late, the bell had gone already. I pointed out the time.

Not yet, she said, there was yet another relationship she wanted to call to my attention, and that was the relationship to pain. When pain made itself felt during an experiment – like now, with this headache – one should never just break off and walk away from it. Instead one should turn upon it the light of awareness.

That is how she spoke. The light of awareness.

And so we turned upon the fear.

Biehl had written his memoirs, *In Grundtvig's Footsteps*. It contained the names of all the teachers who had ever occupied positions at the school, all the moves to bigger and better premises, a long string of achievements and the rewards for them.

But not one word about the relationship to the pupils, and so nothing either about the fear. Not one word, not even in the pauses or in the spaces between the lines.

At first it was impossible to understand. Because that was the truly significant factor. Not the respect, not the admiration. But the fear.

Later it became clear that this reticence was part of the more far-reaching plan. And then I understood.

We stood stock-still during Assembly. That was the first thing I tried to get through to her.

At a certain time every day you were let in to the assembly hall, two hundred and forty people with twenty-six teachers plus Biehl, and then the doors were shut, and you knew that from this moment and for the next quarter of an hour you had to stay dead still.

The prohibition was total, giving rise therefore to a certain tension in the room. As though the rule, by covering everything and by tolerating nothing, called for its own violation. As though the tension in the room were part of the plan.

Over the years it had proved impossible to have the rule observed absolutely. But those few violations that had occurred had, in fact, only served to confirm and reinforce the rule.

Those few times it happened, there had been a faint commotion among the pupils, a hemming and a hawing, and a rustling that spread like an infection and, for a while, could not be stopped. A critical situation, one of the most difficult for a man in Biehl's position. The passive resistance of a great body of small people.

On these occasions he had been brilliant. He did not try to pre-
tend that nothing had happened. He bowed his head and took the
disturbance upon himself. He stood like that, head bowed, while
the tension in the room rose, and eventually the fear stifled the
disturbance.

At no time had he looked directly at anyone; he carried on with
Assembly as usual. Even so, you knew that he knew who had started it.
That he had located the source, and knew how it should be stopped.

Another teacher, who should have been there, never came. Instead,
the door to the classroom stood open, and we waited for a pause
so long that what we had known all along was confirmed for us.
Then Biehl came in, very quick and brisk.

"Sit down," he said, "Jes – remain standing."

He needed some time to get into his stride. Not much, even
though it felt that way after I became ill, probably only a couple
of minutes. Just long enough to go over what had happened. That
Jes had disrupted Assembly for his schoolfellows, disrupted a school
timetable that was already overstretched, abused the trust put in
him and, suddenly, the blow fell.

Very fast, and yet with a weight that jolted the body free of the
desk and out into the aisle.

Just after it struck there was a brief pause and, even though this
was what held the key to the fear, it was so brief that it went
unnoticed, I said, don't talk about it any more.

"On the contrary," she said. "That's exactly what we do have
to talk about."

So I tried. When the blow fell, first there was a short lull, when
the shock had brought everything to a standstill. Then came two
things at once. The relief that everything had now been put to
rights, and something else – something deeper, far-reaching – that
occurs when an adult hits a child hard, something that has nothing
further to do with the pain from the blow.

Back by the blackboard Biehl adjusted his dress. Like a man who
has been to the toilet. Or with a hooker. And has now put behind
him something that was difficult but necessary.

*   *   *

5

She did not understand me, so we went on.

"How often does it happen?" she asked.

Before my illness there had been no reason to wonder about how often. But now, when it was necessary to be aware of time all the time, it turned out to be very seldom, less than once a week in any one class. Quite precisely administered.

"How come?"

It was rather soon to begin initiating her into the inner truths, but I did it anyway. There was a law, it was Karin Ærø who had given this away, that dated from antiquity. When gilding a surface it was not desirable to cover it one hundred per cent with gold. On the contrary, one achieved the best effect if one covered just over sixty per cent. A variation on the law of the golden mean.

So it was, too, with the relationship between time and punishment. Of those violations that were proven, only just over half elicited punishment.

A golden mean of violence, as it were.

How many times had I myself been hit?

To this I was able to reply in the negative, as far as my time here at the school – that is, two years and two months – was concerned; in all that time, until recently, I had never once been hit or been given detention nor, until I became ill, so much as a reprimand or an L for Late.

"No," she said, "when you are scared enough maybe it is even a sort of freedom not to be punished."

She did not mean any harm by it. It just slipped out. It was more or less directed at herself. But it gave away the fact that she felt, for me, an instinctive aversion. And since I had nothing to lose I remarked that – before Biehl's, in my past life, especially at Himmelbjerg House and the Royal Orphanage – I had taken and dished out more than most. She would maybe have been hard put, here at the school, to find a greater specialist in the field of rattled jaws. Short of having gone to Biehl himself.

She asked what he would have said to that.

*   *   *

6

There had been a case at the school a year earlier. A pupil – it was Jes Jessen with whom I had shared a room and who later was expelled – had allegedly suffered a hearing impairment after being punished by Biehl.

It was never proved that the two things had anything to do with one another, but on that occasion Biehl was pushed very close to giving an explanation. He had said that the school, as far as was possible, respected the ban on corporal punishment generally in force in Danish primary schools but, in his experience, a cuff round the ear had never done anyone any harm.

It was said so deeply, that everyone breathed a sigh of relief. He certainly did have experience, after all he had been hitting children regularly for forty years.

At the same time, it was not untrue. It was not the blow itself which was of primary importance, but what happened around it, just before and just after. But which was not usually visible, not to the naked eye. Because it was over so quickly. But still, it went on for a very long time afterwards.

To describe this fleeting, but profound, effect she suggested the word "abasement", which I accepted. So she had, after all, understood.

2

THE EXTERNAL DATA, I mean that outside of the laboratory, was at all times easily accessible.

In the month of May 1971, after almost two years at the school, two years during which no one was able to point the finger at me for anything; when it had been recorded in my file that I was well adjusted and of average intelligence, all of a sudden it became hard for me to be on time in the mornings. On Saturdays and Sundays, when the others were at home and I was alone at the school, I slept during the day or not at all, and was awake at night, and it affected the rest of the week.

I consulted the school doctor, so as not to arouse any suspicion of laziness or lack of zeal, and so that it might be established that this was an illness one could not, oneself, do anything about, not even with two alarm clocks, one of which was pretty big.

The school was under the remit of the district medical officer. He prescribed that I should be woken every morning by Flakkedam, and for a while I did turn up on time, but very tired. At that point I had seen the grand plan, and I began to fear a catastrophe.

That is why I sent the letter. It was the first letter of my life, there never having been anyone to write to.

I had seen her in the playground, with Biehl, under SOLI DEO GLORIA.

Biehl always stood under the inscription over the arch in the morning, to greet those who turned up on time, and to identify those who came late. From the moment one started to wake up one remembered that he would be standing there. So that, in a way, he was already present, between one's dreaming and one's waking.

One had no contact with the other classes; the senior classes, especially, were far away; she was two classes above me. At one point she had been absent, for six months maybe. When she came back she was a boarder, no one knew why. At that time I had seen her, but still only from afar.

One morning I saw her in the playground, she was late, it seemed wrong, she was not the type.

When she was there again, a couple of days later, I began to count; over fourteen school days I counted her six times. Then I knew that something was wrong.

The sixth time, Biehl had drawn her aside.

He had taken her over to the wall, and allowed everyone else to slip past. He was bending over her. He was concentrating hard. This offered the possibility of getting close, so one could see their faces. She was leaning forward a bit, towards him, and she was looking straight at him. I was close enough to see her eyes. It was as though she were looking for something.

Then the thought came to me that we might be of benefit to one another.

A long time passed without my hearing anything. In the end I was close to giving up. I had found her in the class pictures in the school yearbooks, her name was Katarina. One day, on the way to Assembly, she was right behind me on the stairs.

"Library," she said.

It was the first time I heard her voice. She said just the one word.

There was a prohibition against remaining in the school buildings after the bell had gone, the only exception was the library, which was next to the staff room. One could sit there in the lunch break if one wanted to improve one's mind.

Now it was empty, apart from Katarina and me.

She sat for a long while trying to bring herself to say something.

"I do it on purpose," she said. "I come late on purpose."

That had been obvious before in the playground. When Biehl closed in on anyone, they would try to lean away. It just happened, it was a rule. She had leaned towards him, and looked him in the eye. As if to make the most of the moment.

She read aloud from a piece of paper. It looked like a letter.

" 'Apart from the bit about sleep and about concentrating, there are also other things that have not been mentioned to anyone. Whole days that go missing, and fleeting moments that become like an eternity.'

"Tell me about it," she said.

Now, not that I wanted to deny anything, but whoever had written that letter, I said, was definitely taking a big risk, admitting to being so ill. What do you suppose we could do to reduce this risk? Might he perhaps receive some information in return?

"I am conducting an experiment," she said.

That is the sort of thing she said. Conducting an experiment.

"Is there any guarantee that one will turn up on time afterwards?" I said.

To this she said no.

If she had promised anything I would not have believed her, and so it would not have been possible to proceed. But now she was speaking the truth, so I tried.

The first thing I tried to explain to her was Assembly; it was because of a law that Karin Ærø had revealed.

It was not normal for Karin Ærø to speak. Normally she started people off on a song and then walked along the rows to hear who sang true and who sang out of tune, and in this way decide who was in the choir, who was out, and who was on the borderline. But while she listened, sometimes she also spoke, and what she said then was often very important; one of the profound laws for example – like the one about the golden mean.

On one such occasion, she had said that the beginning of a piece of music, if it were an intelligent and precise piece, in very short order invariably determined the rest of its content and course.

Exactly as with Assembly. In shortened form it contained the rest of the day. All the way through school. Maybe for life.

That is why I began there, but at first it was not possible. It seemed unthinkable that she could ever understand, because she was a girl, but mostly because she was on the inside, and had always taken time for granted.

Then the bell rang.

She had no wristwatch, one could not help but notice. But that was not what was most important. What was most important was that she did not hear the bell.

Me it took by surprise, but I heard it.

She did not hear it. Because she was listening to me. So she did not have all the answers in advance.

So I told her about Assembly and the fear. While time passed and the risk of our being discovered grew.

3

BIEHL'S ACADEMY was a reward after the third attempted rape, which was made against me.

At that time I was at the Royal Children's Home at 109 Strand-vejen. It was also known as The Thorup Institute, but the pupils called it Crusty House because of the crusts they had to make do with instead of proper bread.

After it happened – because Valsang, who did it, was a teacher at the school and because there was so much at the back of it – the school board were most concerned and I decided to bring some pressure to bear upon them.

At that point it had become clear that this was not a good place to stay; Oscar Humlum (who had saved me in the telephone box and was my only friend, who had also come from a Home) had been there a year longer than I had. He only survived by taking money for eating various things. It was one crown for an earth-worm and five crowns for a frog, so it was obvious where it was leading.

At that point I had had my first difficulties with time and, on the evening of the day on which he had saved me, I tried to tell him that time, at the school, was being pulled downwards in a spiral. Since we were now both witnesses we should try to make a deal with them so that we could both get away.

It was as though he did not understand me. He dreamed of being a cook on the Swedish ferries, I thought maybe he imagined they had found him a place as an apprentice. He did not answer me, he just shook his head. Nor did he say anything later on, in the office, but he did bring some pressure to bear on them just by being there. They promised they would try to get me into Biehl's Academy which, now and again in recent years, had taken in children with

12

behavioural difficulties from the Homes, and which had a good reputation.

This I told Katarina during our second conversation in the library, the one during which they found us and separated us.

"I can remember when you came," she said. "You were pretty small."

In reply I explained that when I was transferred to Primary V at Biehl's Academy and then put down a class, I weighed twenty-three kilos with clothes, but without shoes. I was at that time one hundred and twenty-eight centimetres, and the district medical officer declared that I was not defective, but that it all had to do with the meals at Crusty House being less than adequate. Besides which, the pecking order had been such that those who had come to the school last – the children from the Homes – were below everybody else, even the day pupils, and got served last in the middle of the day when there was hot food. This, in due course, made it hard because this was the big meal that one was supposed to survive on, through the night too.

At Biehl's Academy, therefore, in that first year I grew twenty-five centimetres and put on seventeen kilos. Even though this resulted in rather a lot of pain in my bones and also fever, in those days I was never absent.

She read aloud from the letter in her hand: " 'Fleeting moments that become like an eternity.' " She asked me to explain it.

Why did it say that?

Well, one had no language of one's own when one came to Crusty House. At Himmelbjerg House and the other Homes before that, one had got by with very few words.

During the first six months one said not a word in class. At the end of that time one had learned the basics. At Biehl's it was well and truly driven home.

One adopted their language, that of the teachers and the schools, one had none of one's own. At first it was like a release, like a key, like a road. The only road in.

Much later one discovers that what one was let into, at that time, was a tunnel. From which one can never again escape. Not entirely. Not in this life.

" 'Fleeting moments that become like an eternity.' What can he have meant?" she said. "The one who wrote the letter."

What was meant was that time is something you have to hold on to and the place where we examined it that first time was where the Hornbæk line ran through the school grounds.

It was Oscar Humlum who discovered it. At that time, I thought it was a game, later I understood that he was ill, that we were both ill.

He played at letting his mind go blank.

Crusty House was a school for academically gifted children who had got into difficulties because they had lacked a firm structure. Because they came from broken homes or maybe alcoholic homes. The school then established the structure that had been lacking. Like, for example, the way you slept in the dormitory, between two sheets and a blanket tucked in under the mattress; two windows open all year round and only one extra blanket in winter.

Most people could, after a while, put up with the most unbelievable things. It kept on, for a long time, being hard for me because I was inadequately fed.

I found out that you could sneak out to the toilet; there was a radiator turned on in there. You waited till the teacher on duty and the other boys were asleep, then you crept out and settled down against the radiator and went to sleep. One night Humlum was sitting there when I came out, he had brought his blanket with him and he was asleep. It was the first time I had really noticed him.

Sometimes we sat for a bit and talked before we fell asleep. We sat, each on our own toilet, with a partition between. Still, we could hear each other even when talking softly. It was there he told me that he played at letting his mind go blank.

We hung a rope from a tree overlooking the railway line, so we could swing out in front of the engine when it came, and hang for a moment outside the windscreen and look in at the engine driver and be away so late that it was clear that one had only just survived.

Normally you would, right through the swing, be thinking how you had to get away in time. Now we tried, instead, to let our minds go blank; to, as it were, switch off, and feel the train, and the rope between our hands, and then it became a very rich moment; then time began to stretch, so that afterwards one could not say how long it had lasted. In the longest moments, those two times when I was brushed by the train, there had been no time at all.

Even then one sensed that it must be a rule. That time could not be something that passed all by itself but was something one had to hold on to. And that, when one let go of it, that moment was very significant.

In a way this discovery was a help. But at the same time that was, in fact, the illness.

This I told Katarina while she listened.

At Crusty House no one had ever listened, at any rate no adults.

No harm intended. The school had established the firm structure that people had lacked. Anker Jørgensen had gone there, the school had reared a prime minister.

Even though that was not the norm. The norm was, that of the fifteen who came into a new class, approximately half would have to leave within the first four years, because they could not cope with the academic side; or just could not cope.

I was only twelve when I was moved, but even then it was obvious that, for most of those who were left, things did not look good. Most of them were lost.

The Hornbæk line's own people, together with the fire brigade, came and felled the tree. I was under suspicion, but it was the day

15

before I was to leave the school, and they wanted to avoid attracting any attention, so they did not pursue the case.

I dried up there. I felt very empty. It was necessary for her to say something in return.

At Crusty House we had three kroner a month dished out and three saved; even so, one paid what one owed, it was an absolute rule, even to Gummi who could go without for a very long time and held on to sweets till the end of the month and sold them dear. The few times it happened that someone tried to get out of it they were made to jump from the willow tree down into the lake. It was a ten-metre drop, but only one metre of water. You did not break anything, but you sank into mud up to your chest and then you were sucked down slowly and only pulled out after your hair had been under for a while.

So you always gave something in return and paid what you owed. Everybody did. It was an absolute rule.

Katarina must have known this. First she waited for me to go on, but I said nothing. I could not. Then she said:

"By the way, both my mother and my father died last year."

At Crusty House I had tried to imagine what it was like to be with a family. You imagined that you were walking along Strandvejen, and one of the kitchen maids came cycling along. She stopped and took you up behind her on her bike, and you talked freely and openly, and cycled home to where she lived. It was a house, and her father and mother were there, and you sat down at the dinner table and there was loads of food. That, more than anything, was how one imagined a family. That there was enough food.

When Katarina referred to her mother and father for the first time, you could hear that there was something else, too. At first you did not understand what.

She never said what their home had been like, not one word. Still, I could picture it. There had been books and lamps and parquet flooring – easily damaged, but no one shouted at you, even if you spilled something, it was just mopped up, because that sort of thing can happen to anyone.

"They often talked about time," she said.

They had talked about time, there had been nothing strange about that, it had been altogether normal. Although not so much about time by a clock, but more about time out in space. Katarina had heard them talking about whether it passed forwards or backwards.

Then her mother had become very ill. The doctors had said that she had less than three months to live and it was then that she had become interested in ordinary time.

"She developed a scientific theory," said Katarina.

Why scientific?

This was the first time I heard that word used about a thought that an ordinary person had had. Why was it important that the theory was scientific, for her mother, and after that for Katarina, and after that for me and August?

Maybe there are only two kinds of question in the world.

The kind they ask in school, where the answer is known in advance; not asked so that anyone will be any the wiser, but for other reasons.

And then the others, those in the laboratory. Where one does not know the answers, and often not even the question, before one has asked it.

Questions like what is time; why Oscar Humlum said, Save yourself; and why Axel Fredhøj lay down beside the lagging.

Questions that are quite painful. And that are not asked until one is driven to it. Like when they gave her mother three months.

That was what we meant by science. That both question and answer are tied up with uncertainty, and that they are painful. But that there is no way round them. And that one hides nothing; instead everything is brought out into the open.

"She began to think that time only passed when one was unaware," said Katarina.

Her mother had begun to believe that time sort of stole forwards, in jerks, when one's mind was elsewhere. That the bit about her only having three months left was on the basis that she did not concentrate. Then she became very aware.

17

It pretty soon became wearisome. She stopped sleeping at night, and Katarina and her father did not sleep much either, but when they did finally sleep they would wake up to find her mother sitting looking at them, so as not to miss a single second.

When the three months were up she had felt sure that she was now living a life of total awareness and had more or less stopped time, and she took Katarina with her on some of her visits to the hospital.

"The doctors sat," said Katarina, "and she walked back and forth and told them that the passage of time was just carelessness. She weighed less than forty kilos and had no hair left on her head."

Eighteen months later she was dead. She had refused to take pills. Said that they took the edge off, that, rather, one should turn upon the pain the light of awareness.

Katarina had started to walk back and forth in front of the windows. She may have meant to tell me about her father too, but no longer felt up to it.

"I saw them both afterwards," she said; "there were only six months between them. It wasn't them. It *was* them, but there was no more life in them. That was gone. It isn't something you normally think about, that there is life in a person. But when one knows them and how they ought to be, then one understands something. That life cannot just go away. That it must have gone somewhere. So I formed a hypothesis."

She walked over to me.

"She tried to stretch the seconds by sort of staring at them. And he tried, afterwards, to shorten them, to make them pass more quickly. They cannot have been living in the same time. They must each have had their own, different from the one that the rest of the world went by. Afterwards, time became different for me too. Often I thought: Now things are as bad as they can get, and will stay that way for ever. Like you wrote: 'Moments that become like an eternity'. When I saw them lying there, I knew it. That there is not just one time, that there must be different sorts of time, all existing at once."

She was now talking so quietly that I had to lean forward. It was not out of fear – I think she had forgotten how close we were to the staff room – it was because this was so important to her that it was hard to say.

"I want to study it scientifically," she said. "We're going to try to touch time."

To touch time. That, I suppose, is what life for me has been about since then.

This is the laboratory. It is next to the bedroom, where the child and the woman are sleeping. I am afraid.

Once, I thought what I feared was that something would separate me from the child. But it is not that. What I am afraid of is that the world and the child will never be part of one another; I mean, that the child will die. Or the world. I would do anything, no matter what, to avoid that.

That sounds so totally inadequate. But I cannot put it any better.

The fear for oneself, that one can do something about. On it one can turn the light of awareness. But when one is no longer worrying about oneself, then comes the fear for other people, and after that, for the world.

There are no fearless people, only fearless moments. Like those here in the laboratory. During and after the work there is a kind of peace.

Katarina would have told me about her father too, but she did not get the chance. We must both have missed hearing the bell, and this time word had gone out to look for us.

It was Fredhøj who came. He remained standing for a while in the doorway, stock-still, and looked at us. Then he stepped aside and we walked out.

4

BIEHL'S ACADEMY had a good name. It had always been said that the school set a high academic standard.

Even so, now and again, they took in the occasional backward pupil, one who, for example, required special tuition. In due course, these pupils were raised to the same standard as the rest.

This was common knowledge, it was part of the thinking behind the school.

In recent years they had, moreover, taken in pupils for whom special circumstances came into play. For this there was no explanation.

That was how I got in. And August, too.

He started on 3 October. By that time Katarina and I had, as a precautionary measure, not spoken for one week and two days.

I saw him in the morning, in first period, in Biehl's office. I had been summoned. Biehl was there, and Fredhøj and Flakkedam. August was standing in front of Flakkedam. He was a head shorter than me.

"This is August," said Biehl.

Then Flakkedam ushered him out.

Biehl was holding his dossier.

"He has had an accident," he said, "since which he has trouble remembering things. He will be in your class. You will sit next to him."

Something was afoot, their faces were very aware.

"He lost his father," said Biehl; "his mother is still in hospital. It is not to be spoken of."

Just as I was going out of the door, he put the dossier back.

You knew that the files existed, and that there was one for each pupil. But you did not know where they were kept, nor would I have known now, but one could not help but see it.

A wooden chest, with the school crest carved on its lid – Hugin and Munin, Odin's ravens. Each morning they fly out from Valhalla and in the evening return to perch on Odin's shoulders and whisper in his ears of all that they have seen.

The open lid of the chest was facing me as I stepped through the doorway. You could not help but notice that it had only a straightforward three- or four-tumbler furniture lock.

One's eye was caught, too, by the ravens. They had taken on the look of birds of prey.

That was not the intention. The intention had been that one should think of the ravens as being like children and young people of school age, gathering knowledge and experience, which they would then practise faithfully in their relationship to their superiors. Then, too, there was the birds' flight and the Nordic myths. It was a brilliant image.

Still, one could not, at that moment when Biehl put August's papers back into the chest, avoid the thought that these two ravens stood also for surveillance and control. And, in due course, punishment or reward.

That very day I came into contact with Katarina.

There were two hundred and forty pupils at the school. No more. This, in order to maintain both the academic standard and close contact between teachers and pupils.

This meant that most of the teachers knew almost all of the pupils, it was very difficult to escape notice. Even at a place like Himmelbjerg House, where there had been a matron and a deputy and six assistants and a social worker and a nurse and a janitor for twenty-four pupils, because we were so damaged, not even there had the supervision been as good as at Biehl's. It was very difficult to be alone.

The only time when it was hard for them to avoid disintegration was when you were going from one place to another. Like just after the bell had gone.

Two teachers monitored the ascent to the classrooms; one under the archway and one halfway up the stairs between the first and second floors, from where they could see almost everything – not, however, the stairs between the ground floor and the first floor. There I met Katarina.

On the landing, in one corner, there was a seat – triangular, screwed on to the wall. If you stood up against it you were invisible to the guards, and did not get swept along in the stream of pupils making their way upwards.

"I have to talk to you," she said. "You were about to tell me about the Orphanage."

She was talking as though we had just been interrupted. We stood close together, there was nothing special to tell about that time, I just shook my head.

She leaned towards me. Around us people were making their way up. The noise was overwhelming. She did not let it bother her.

"There was the bit about my father," she said.

I did not want to hear it, but she told me anyway.

"He could not bear the fact that she wasn't there any more. He hanged himself. Well?"

I wouldn't know what to say about that, I said, but what about those one leaves behind, what about them, how are they to manage, who's going to think of them?

"Have you never left anyone?" she said. "Your friend from back then, do you ever see him? Why didn't he come here too?"

She meant Humlum. We were alone on the stairs now, soon we would be missed.

I did not mean to tell her, but I did anyway, for no special reason.

Other than that she listened, and that it just came out. There was nothing to be done about it.

At the Orphanage, after school, we had our set tasks, that is to say: kitchen duty, emptying the bins, odd jobs in the house and in the garden, as well as special duties. One of the special duties was cutting Valsang's grass.

As a rule one was not offered this until Primary VI; he asked me halfway through Primary V, six months before I was transferred.

Up there one was allowed to take stuff from his fridge, it was absolutely legal. One went up after school and cut the grass and ate from the fridge.

The next thing that happened was that he said one could stay the night there, and one accepted. It was never talked about, not even among the pupils. One stayed the night up there. No one had ever come to any harm.

At first I did not want to, but it was something everyone had to go through.

He taught Danish. In the evening he played music for me on his record player, then I went into the spare room where he had made up the bed. The cramps started while I was lying waiting for him to come, they had been there before, just not so bad. Then time began to float. I did not know whether a minute or an hour had passed. It was there it became clear to me that I was ill.

In the end I left before he came. He had locked me in, but it was only an inside lock, a piece of bent wire will open them.

From then on I knew that I was too weak to make it at the school.

After that he was very much on the alert. Not angry, just very often near at hand. Twice, in the showers, he very nearly got me.

There was no one to talk to about it, it was not the sort of thing one could bring up. All the others had been there, Humlum too, and none of them had come to any harm.

I'm getting to it now.

I was passing the telephone box. It was on the first floor. It was in the afternoon. He opened the door and pulled me in and pushed me up against the shelf with the telephone books. He asked me to look up a number, he had forgotten his reading glasses.

It's no good. Going on. It was no good, not even with Katarina. I cannot say it – not just yet – I have to say something else first.

We struggled to get top marks for discipline, that was the ultimate goal, better than getting on to the school team, better than being seen with one of the kitchen maids.

For most people, the school was their last chance, they knew they were all but lost. They had no family, or they had been latchkey kids from the age of five, or they were like Gummi who had not even been given a key but had to sleep on the doormat and had had pneumonia so many times that sport and standing up for himself were now out of the question, so he only survived because he could hide his sweets and sell them dear at the end of the month. Crusty House was the last resort, after that came a treatment home and that was that.

They had been given the chance because they were academically gifted. Now it was a matter of hanging on. So one sat there, with graph paper and two jotters, and copybook-writing even when it was just sums done in ink. What one was mapping out was the structure that had not been firm enough, and which one now had to keep within. With precision and accuracy. This was the last and only chance.

Like looking things up accurately. We had had exercises in using telephone directories; that was in Valsang's classes.

I tried to look it up, I really tried. Even though I knew it was just something he had said, I really tried. Even though he had opened his fly and had his chopper out, and the tension inside the box grew and the cramps started.

One cannot keep running away. There seemed to be nothing else for it but to try to hold him off, while turning the pages with the other hand, as one had been asked.

The door of the box was of matte glass in a steel frame. Valsang held it closed with his free hand. Humlum smashed it with a fire extinguisher. They were topped up with water once a year, they held forty litres, plus the weight of the metal.

It was safety glass, it sort of disintegrated and covered us in gritty dust.

There were a fair number of pupils outside, maybe thirty or forty. A couple of the bigger ones looked damaged. They had refused to come because it was something to do with Valsang. Humlum had forced them, so that there would be witnesses. They did not want to look, they tried to look away. Even so, they had to look at us.

They stood absolutely still. There was a narrow space between them and the telephone box which we came out through, first Valsang and me, then Humlum with the fire extinguisher. Slowly they followed us. We went into the office.

In the ordinary time, that of a watch, one understands certain, specific things. When one lets go of time one understands certain other things.

This was the alternative which illness offered. When something important was happening, one could let go, and achieve a rich moment, full of understanding. It is like moving in on a black hole. If one gets too close, one gets sucked in. But if one comes up alongside it, there is understanding.

While we were still making for the office, the thought occurred that we ought to be able to use this, to get something in return. That we could bring pressure to bear upon them, and get away.

This I told Katarina. While we were alone on the stairs.

"So why didn't he come with you?" she asked.

"He didn't want to," I said. "When it came right down to it he just said, 'Save yourself.' "

She asked if I still saw him.

"He comes to visit me," I said. "But in secret."

IN CLASS WE SAT, divided into three rows, facing the teacher's desk. Farthest away, in the window row, in the light, there were just girls. In the middle row both girls and boys, in the door row just boys.

Here they had cleared three desks. The middle one was for August and me.

In front of us and behind us there were empty desks. Flakkedam sat down at the empty desk behind us.

A number of rules had been imposed on August. It took me a while to work out what they were. He was forbidden to get to his feet without permission, or to make any sudden movements. On those occasions when he did so anyway Flakkedam was onto him like a shot.

So we sat, on our own, with empty desks in front and behind, right over beside the wall. He was also forbidden to move. One could not help but think that he had, at one and the same time, both less and more space than anyone else in the school.

No explanation was given.

Biehl's Academy was a fee-paying school.

It was common knowledge that they were very particular about the appointment of new teachers. There were always a lot of applicants, each and every one of whom was called in for an exhaustive interview. But Fredhøj, who was deputy head, had told us during one class that certain applicants had been rejected before the interview, while still in the secretary's office, because they had looked scruffy, or had not been there at the appointed time. After a series of interviews, one candidate was selected for the vacant position.

This was important for the school. That the teachers were highly qualified and carefully chosen.

It was more or less the same in the case of the pupils. Something that was mentioned pretty often was the waiting lists.

For every single class the school had a waiting list. It was so long that at any given time they could have doubled the number of pupils. This did not happen. It was part of Grundtvig's philosophy that schools should be kept rather small. Besides which, it was a prerequisite of the high academic standard.

What happened with the waiting lists was that they were just there. Then, when it was necessary to request a pupil's parents to remove the person concerned from the school, or if something else happened, then that place was filled from the list.

Up to eighteen. Where, in an ordinary state school, there could be as many as thirty-six pupils in each class, at Biehl's there were only eighteen. It was a prerequisite of the standard.

The waiting lists meant that the school was under no pressure to keep any pupil. This was something everyone knew, that there was no reason for the school to keep anyone. As to its being a fee-paying school, Fredhøj had said this ensured that it was those parents with a special and more serious interest in their children who put them into the school. But to ensure that it was also open to poor families with academically gifted children, there was the possibility of applying for a full or partial scholarship.

So the pupils were selected by way of their parents' loving care. And outside each class, on the lists, at least eighteen others were in line to take their places – we all knew that.

Which is why it was hard to see why they let in August.

It was like a sign.

Why did they take him?

It was hard enough to understand it with a character like Carsten Sutton. Or me, who was just of average intelligence or a bit below, and on a scholarship, and who was starting to come to class very late, even though they did not yet know how bad things had become.

But that they should take August was inexplicable. When they had the waiting lists and had no need to keep anyone. Why did they take someone like him?

It was this question that made me sure there had to be a plan. But long before then, more than once, one had noticed things.

The first sign came after a year at the school, when we received word about the covert Darwinism. When it came, the word, it made one's previous life as clear as daylight.

Oscar Humlum and I had been travelling companions for a long time before we met, though without knowing it.

There was nothing strange about this. It was perfectly normal. Because, for an orphan in Denmark, everything was very strictly regulated. Across the country ran certain tunnels that were invisible; they ran alongside each other, absolutely parallel. So, when Humlum and I met, we did not talk much about the past. This silence – it was so as not to pry, but also because we knew that, in a way, we had been travelling together, even though we had not seen one another.

First one was put into a Home for Infants. One was so small, there, that one could not remember anything, but the file stated that I had been in two different ones.

After that, one was put in a children's home. Both Humlum and I had been with the Christian Foundation. I was at the Home on Peter Bang's Vej, between the KB playing fields and Flintholm Church. Humlum was in Esbjerg. One feels as though one ought to have remembered quite a bit about that time, but the only thing one remembered was the storytelling, and the punishment for soiling one's mouth with swearwords – the matron, Sister Ragna, pushed one's head down the toilet after she had used it.

One ought to have remembered more. But that was the only thing that had stuck.

They kept you for as long as they could at the children's home. Only if they came to the conclusion that there was no alternative were you moved. There was only one kind of place to go to from there. That was to a residential assessment centre, for a limited period. I went to Brogårdsvænge in Gentofte, that was in '66. I remember nothing about why, in the file, the matron, Sister Ragna, had written "wayward, refuses to wear plus-fours".

That is what it says, but one remembers nothing.

One time I showed it to Humlum. It was winter, at night. We were sitting on the toilets, up against the radiator. "I remember them," he said, "baggy pants and long, checked socks. The rest of them at the school wore desert boots and Fair Isle sweaters. You didn't have anything else, it was like your skin, it got to the stage where you wanted to rip it off, rip your skin off, or something."

He did not say whether he too had refused.

It was all downhill from the assessment centre. Because one was older there were more places they could send one. I was put into a boarding school for children whose development does not measure up to the norm, and from there to Nødebogård Treatment Home.

That was in '67, I must have been ten. By then there had been various offences, mostly running away and break-ins, but other things too that I will not mention, even assault.

At that point one was allowed to see bits of one's file, it was all part of the new trend in education at that time. The man from the social-services department showed it to me. It was the first time I saw it. There it stated exactly how things stood: "behavioural disturbances", "problems with adjustment to school", "conduct disorders", "antisocial", "truancy". "What are we to do?" he said. "You will be sent to Nødebogård until a place becomes vacant at an approved school in Jutland."

Approved school was not an official term. Unofficially, though, the meaning was crystal clear. It meant those schools and homes where the staff kept a tight grip on things, and had the experience and the resources to take on even very young offenders. I had been at Nødebogård for two months when a place became vacant at Himmelbjerg House and I was transferred. Humlum and I talked sometimes about how it would have been if he had been transferred at the same time, so we would have met each other at Himmelbjerg House instead of a year later at Crusty House.

But that did not happen, since he had, two years earlier, stopped talking.

In my case they always knew that I was not backward. No one suspected that I might be academically gifted, but no one had ever actually thought that I was retarded. Apparently, in Humlum's case, they had not been so sure. Added to which, he had stopped talking. For a year and a half he said nothing, not one word.

He never did say that much, not even later, not even about why he had stopped talking. All he told me was that his mouth had hurt.

It was true, one could tell just by looking at him. Talking for any length of time hurt. So there came a point when he stopped altogether.

First of all they sent him to a holiday home for assessment purposes, and then to Copenhagen, where the child-psychiatry clinics were. First he was sent to the Juvenile Clinic in Læssøesgade – to ambulatory assessment, where they dealt with the most difficult cases. There he was put down as 3.

When you were "in care" you could be four things, nothing else was possible. You could be "of normal intelligence", that was 1, or "mildly retarded", that was 2. Both 1 and 2 could be with or without "general adjustment problems". Then you could be 3, like Humlum, who had "social adjustment problems with neurotic or other pathological characteristics"; 4 was "feeble-minded or severely retarded".

3 was very dangerous. If you had been in an approved school and a treatment home for the mildly retarded and if they concluded that one fell into the lowest level for 3, or lower, there was only one alternative, and that was mental retardation services. On the bottom rung of mental retardation services came permanent residential care, in a locked ward, strapped down and three injections daily.

Still, Humlum went along with it of his own free will, and got himself put down as 3. He told me he had had a nice time. They had examined him on Mondays and Wednesdays, but apart from that they left him alone. He only went to school two days a week and was put on a special diet, with dessert after meals and seconds if he asked for them.

I never worked out just how long this went on for, a year and a half at least. He attended the Save the Children child psychiatry out-patients clinic, and finally the child-psychiatry clinic at Copenhagen University, where they assessed him as being below the limit for feeble-minded, 4 that is, and then he got scared and started talking again. Then it was recommended that he be transferred to the Central Mission reception centre for retarded children on Gersonsvej in Hellerup. To get out of this he made a great effort. Then they realised that he was academically gifted and he was sent, instead, to sit an entrance exam for the Home. "I had to do my best," he said. He passed and was accepted, a year before me.

By not talking for so long he had discovered the thing about letting your mind go blank. He told me that this had been the only time ever when he could sleep properly at night, the world had become different. "Time," he said, "began to flow, like when you let your mind go blank."

He was the first one to suggest that there must be a plan. In a way all the homes were alike. Some had locks; some had one sort of workshop, while others had another sort. With all of them it was as though they were saturated by tight, tight time.

I had noticed this, but had not been able to put it into words. Humlum did.

"There must be a plan," he said, "why else should it be so important to be so precise, eh?"

I just listened, I had nothing to say.

"When you let your mind go blank," he said, "or when you stop talking for a long time, something happens. Time becomes different. It goes away. It doesn't come back until you start to say something."

*   *   *

31

After he said that, it was three years before anyone talked about time. That was in the laboratory, when Katarina said that we were going to study it.

By then it was a year since Biehl had given the signal, and revealed the plan for helping the borderline cases.

It came at a time when it had become hard to see any way out.

At Crusty House there had been compulsory home visits every third weekend, on these occasions they sent me to Høve to the holiday home for underprivileged children. That did not work out very well. The place was used for the assessment of children from Copenhagen who had been in gangs that had been split up. At the home they formed new gangs – they were used to working like that. When I left there the last time they had knocked out four of my bottom teeth and I had been abused sexually. I was given silver teeth. I refused to go back there.

At Biehl's I saw a chance to get out of it. I went for it in a lunch break. I wrote a letter to myself from my guardian on one of the typewriters they used for teaching from the leaving-certificate class up. It said that I was invited to visit her at her home. I presented it and was given permission. I left for Copenhagen on the Friday evening, after we had eaten. You could do whatever you wanted – follow people or just walk the streets unhindered – it was brilliant. At night you just went back to the school.

Still, I could not sleep. I do not know why, I just could not. Sometimes a whole weekend would go past without my getting a wink of sleep. On Monday morning one was very tired and it affected the rest of the week.

It is not true, what I said about those weekends. Often one did not go into town. Often one just stood there, down at the gate, watching the cars driving past. The school and the annexe were deserted, people were at home, I was the only one left. That was not so good.

The next week one was unprepared and numb inside.

Then came the signal.

*   *   *

It came in biology class. Biehl explained about Darwinism – the survival of the fittest. "It still applies," he said, "even in our society, but it is mitigated because we alleviate its consequences."

After he had said that there was a pause. It was a rich moment.

He had not looked at anyone in particular. He never addressed himself, as it were, to individuals. Still, maybe I was the one, at that moment, who understood him best.

Those who were on the inside, the majority that is, for them it had been hard to get his point, mostly they were just pleased that they were on the inside, that they were the fittest.

For those on the outside, the fear and the abandonment amounts to almost everything; everybody knows that.

Understanding is something one does best when one is on the borderline.

It was a law, that was what one understood. It selected some, and some it tumbled into perdition. But for those on the borderline work was being done to alleviate the consequences. For them there was a chance. Biehl's Academy was that chance.

Understanding that is something one does best when one is declared a borderline case.

Biehl very rarely came to a halt. But when he had said this, he had come to a halt. It had not been planned. It was an involuntary stoppage. We were close to something crucial.

"Listen to my pauses. They speak louder than my words."

The covert Darwinism. The plan behind time was selection. Time was a tool that made the selection. One experienced a great sense of relief because everything had been cleared up.

Only much later, when I met Katarina, did the thought strike me that something had been left unexplained.

6

WHAT IS TIME? I shall have to try to say, but not yet. It is too overwhelming for that. You have to begin more simply.

What does it mean – to measure time? What is a timepiece?

Fredhøj had a watch, and looked at it often. Biehl had a fob watch, I never saw him look at it, not once.

Katarina did not have a watch, neither did August, nor did I ever get one. At first, because there was no one to give it to me; later on I never felt like having one.

I have read that they have never made a timepiece that is absolutely precise. No disrespect to science, but no perfectly accurate timepiece has ever been devised. In the course of this century they discovered that the movements of the heavenly bodies were not, as they had previously believed, constant. That the course of the earth's orbit around the sun varied from year to year. So they had to select one particular year, to provide them with a starting point at least. They selected the year 1900. In 1956 the unit of time was redefined by one second to 1/31,556,925.9747 of the tropical year 1900.

Unfortunately that year will never come round again. The earth will never again move exactly as it did in that year, because of earthquakes and other irregularities that have affected its course. This makes it hard to synchronise the world's timepieces. It is hard to set a watch by an event that took place in the previous century.

Which is why, in 1967, they supplemented this definition with atomic time, in which a second corresponds to 9,192,631.770 radiation periods of a particular caesium-133 transition in what they

34

call a caesium clock. Fredhøj told us about it in physics. Now there were two methods of dating accurately, he said, the one supplementing the other.

Later I read that, regrettably, these two systems are always out of step with one another, except for just after they have been synchronised, which has, therefore, to be done continually.

Not meaning to be petty-minded. The most precise atomic timepieces they have constructed so far have shown a day-to-day variation of less than 10^{-8}, which would, over 300,000 years, show up as an error of no more than one second. No one can deny that it is exceedingly accurate. Everyone has done their best.

But, I mean, it is not absolutely precise.

It would not have mattered so much if they had not made such a point of this thing about time. Not that it was ever talked about. Never. Humlum and Katarina were the first people I heard talk about time. But it was at the root of everything. It screwed life down. Like some kind of tool.

It was not just the classes and Assembly that began on the dot. There was also compulsory prep and chores and voluntary sport and lights out and when you had to get up if you were to manage a proper wash, and at what time every third week the green vitamin pills for the next three weeks were dished out and what time on Sunday evenings one had to report back to Flakkedam after weekends at home. Every one of them had been allotted a stroke of the clock that was most scrupulously observed. The inaccuracy amounted to less than plus or minus two minutes.

No explanation of time was ever given. But one knew that it was enormous, bigger than anything mortal or earthly. That you had to be on time was not just out of consideration for your fellow pupils and your own self and the school. It was also for the sake of time itself. For God's sake.

For God's sake.

There had always been a lot of praying and singing. But we had never tried to get through to God himself. For He had always been too close to Biehl or the rector at the Orphanage or the superintendent at Himmelbjerg House. Far too close to let us pray.

To pray is to confess something, to admit that one needs help.

We were afraid that any confession, even to God, could worsen our situation and be used against us.

Grundtvig had written that the day was created for action and the twilight for rest, and that one should, therefore, be precise.

When time itself was so exact, then so ought people to be, that was the idea. Accuracy was a characteristic, and perhaps the most important one, of the universe. At Assembly one had to be absolutely precise and absolutely still. Utter time and utter stillness. That was the goal. Achievement was there to bring us nearer to that goal. And to encourage achievement, there was punishment.

One tried to be totally exact, because time and the world were. One tried and tried all the way through one's adolescence, and one could not, and one came very close to giving up. Yet they had never been able to construct an absolutely accurate timepiece. They had never been able to show that time itself remained constant.

Deep down, they themselves had never managed to be absolutely precise. Nor had they been able to prove that the world is.

$$7$$

FOR THE FIRST WEEK August slept in the sickbay, then he was
moved into my room. Since Jes Jessen had been expelled I had had
it to myself.

At Crusty House, for a few months, they had had a fox. Lent by
Svinninge wildlife park as part of the nature-study programme.
Sometimes Humlum and I would stand in front of its cage. It never
saw us. It looked straight through us and out at the world as it
paced relentlessly back and forth behind the bars. We knew how
it felt. How all its mortal despair at being cooped up had been
compressed into an endless, steady, rhythmic monotony.

August was like that fox.

He got his medicine at nine o'clock, Flakkedam came with two
Mogadon and watched him wash them down with a glass of water,
and then checked with a finger to see that he had not hidden them
under his tongue.

It usually took about three quarters of an hour for them to work.
During that time he was very restless. He paced along the walls
and did not hear you if you spoke to him. Gradually he slowed
down; finally he had to lie down, and he would fall asleep without
saying anything.

I got through to him because I discovered that the key to him
lay in his movements.

On the third day I began pacing beside him, brushing along the
bed and the door and the other bed and under the washbasin and
the window and past the cupboard and then round again, and I
kept going even after he had tried to shake me off, and even though
he looked past me, as the fox had done. At a certain point, just

before he collapsed, I got through to him. By then I had absorbed his restlessness and he had got used to me, and the medicine had taken the edge off his nerves.

For my part, there was nothing personal in this. I did not owe him anything. But he had been entrusted into my care. Not that it had been said in so many words, but he had been linked with me. If he survived and was allowed to stay at the school, at least for a while, it would be to the benefit of us both.

At the start of the sixth night, in the last minutes before he fell asleep, he showed me his drawing. He had it tucked in against his stomach. You could not help but see it, but I had not asked about it. Now he showed it to me all by himself.

He brought it out and unfolded it – a drawing on a large, white sheet of paper, of the kind that was not to be removed from the art class.

It was done in pencil. It was a story. Two little men moved from picture to picture as in a cartoon. It was a chain of violence.

In the drawing, several people got shot, among them a man and a woman in a room. It could have been a living room, or maybe a classroom.

It was hard to look at, but, incredible as it seemed, it was better than the real thing. So he was not useless at everything.

He would have started along the walls again, but the Mogadons were beginning to get to him.

"I didn't get any stars," he said.

Karin Ærø stuck gold paper stars on our art work according to merit. Some people got no stars. A lot got one, some got two. A very few managed three. If you got three stars three times in a row you also received the honour of a brown paper bag full of fruit. In the two years for which this system had been running only Regner Grasten, who went on to become a film producer and very famous, ever got fruit, and only once.

August was now lying down altogether. He was shaking. I tried to understand him – why was it so important? – but it was inexplicable.

"I'm a habitual liar," he said, "the police said so."

"They always say that," I said, "it's absolutely normal, that's what they've always said about me, too."

I did not enquire into what it was he had lied about.

"But the psychologists say I can't remember," he said.

I asked him if he agreed, but he did not answer.

"You should try to fill in the background," I said. "Karin Ærø isn't keen on blank backgrounds. By the time you're finished there should never be too much white paper showing."

8

THE SCHOOL WAS LAID OUT in such a way that the main building – five floors, plus attic rooms – sat between two asphalted playgrounds. The north playground was where you spent the breaks. On the other side of that lay the annexe. Pupils were not allowed in the south playground which was used as a car park by teachers, visitors and delivery vans.

It was surrounded by its grounds, on the edge of which were the teachers' residences. To the south, beyond the gate, was where Copenhagen began.

Across the north playground ran two red lines, one indicating the ten metres around the main school door and one splitting the playground in two.

The latter, apart from being used in the marking out of games pitches, also served to separate those pupils who had been forbidden to talk to one another. To prevent them meeting during breaks, each was assigned to one side of the playground. This made it easy for the teacher on playground duty to see that they stayed apart.

The ten-metre zone ensured a clear area in front of the only exit from the playground. There was a prohibition against leaving the playground during breaks. Anyone who had a go at it anyway had to cross a deserted area and could not help but be noticed by the teacher on duty.

The school building separated the two playgrounds. There was a ban against staying in the building during breaks. At that time there was also a prohibition against leaving the north playground.

The day after August had shown me his drawing Katarina came over to me at the lunch break. Until then we had avoided each other in the playground, where so many people could see us. Now she came right over to me. "Come down to the gym at half-past," she said, "I want to show you something in the south playground."

"That's in the middle of a period," I said.

"The gym will be empty."

She was standing side on, so nobody could see that we were talking.

"The door to the ground floor," I said. "It's locked."

"They deliver the milk next period. It'll be open."

The bell rang. Flage Biehl – he was Biehl's brother – was on playground duty. He was looking around, we had to get away from one another.

She had been wearing a blue sweater. Her hair disappeared into its collar. You have to imagine that she has pulled it over her head, and that her hair has been caught in at the fabric. And she has not pulled it free, just loosened it. Between the fabric and her hair was her neck. Very white. It was a cold day.

Over those two weeks when I had not seen her, except for that time on the stairs, I had had a dream. At night, but when I was awake.

It began just after August became calm and before I fell asleep. There was a forest: pretty dark, very cold, utterly desolate, nothing to eat. Even so, I knew that everything would probably be alright. I had a sleeping bag and a waterproof groundsheet, or an oilskin cape, more like. It was getting late, I spread out the oilskin cape.

Then a girl appeared. She was alone, and cold. I waved to her, keeping my distance so as not to scare her. She was quite clear, but yet she was no one in particular. It would have been too much if she had been someone in particular.

I offered to let her sleep in the sleeping bag while I kept watch. I said it straight out so she would understand that I meant her no harm. She lay down. And then she asked me to lie down beside her. So that we could keep warm. And I did. I lay down beside her, and laced the bag up around our shoulders. Outside the night was cold and very dark. But we were not cold.

The dream ended there. There was no more to it. Nothing else happened. It surfaced while I was separated from her; I had never had it before. Since then it has never left me. I have never told a soul about it before.

*   *   *

Under normal circumstances I could not have left the class. From Primary III up leaving the room during a class was not acceptable. But with August's coming things were a bit different. Even the teachers were affected by it. We had Flage Biehl for arithmetic. I put up my hand and asked leave to go to the toilet, and was given permission without any more ado.

Usually, during a period, you were never anywhere else but in a classroom. The building was unfamiliar then – it seemed abandoned, the sound on the stairs was different, one could be heard from a long way off.

The doors from the stairway to the corridors leading to the classrooms were always locked, but the one on the ground floor was open. She had been right. From the ground floor three steps ran down to the milk cellar, which held the fridges for the milk dished out at lunch break.

The gym was empty, as she had said. She was waiting behind the apparatus. There was a door out on to the south playground. She had it standing ajar.

She was edgy. At first I thought it was from fear of being discovered. But it was not. She had something on her mind.

I asked her about the bit with the milk, and the gym being empty – how had she known?

She showed me a piece of paper. It was a sheet like the one August had taken from the art room.

"I've copied down the timetables for every class in the school," she said. "There is a schedule for every pupil."

She looked out of the door.

"Whose is the car?" she said.

Fredhøj's Rover, Biehl's Volvo and some other teachers' cars were parked in the playground. Beside the secretary's red Mascot sat a grey Taunus – not a teacher's car. That was the one she meant.

"Our class has windows looking on to here," she said. "He comes every Wednesday. I've seen him in the corridor with Biehl. They walk side by side."

Biehl had a particular way of walking. He let people walk ahead of him – pupils far ahead, teachers closer. Flakkedam closer still. The only one he walked alongside was Fredhøj and even they were not exactly abreast.

"It's probably one of the school inspectors," I said.

Now and again they came to sit in on a class and listen. Afterwards Fredhøj would mention that they had, as always, been pleased by the standard of teaching.

"This is the seventh Wednesday running," she said. "I've seen him coming out of the clinic. He talks to both Biehl and Hessen every time."

Just at that moment he emerged from the south stairway. He got into the Taunus and drove away at once. We only saw him from behind.

I tried to get out of telling her, but she leaned towards me, there was no way round it.

"I've seen him once," I said, "at Gladsaxe Stadium, when we beat the Catholic school 3–2. I scored the winning goal. He presented the trophy. His name's Baunsbak-Kold. He's the Director of Education for Copenhagen."

She looked at me, unseeing.

"Could you get into that car without a key?"

I did not answer straight away, my mouth was dry. A person who could ask something like that ran the risk, any minute, of tumbling into perdition.

"No," I said.

This was not true. The car was a Taunus – wafers in both door- and ignition-locks. I said no to protect her, it was for her own good.

"The new boy," she said, "why did they take him?

The first time August had a drawing handed back I had not been there. But the second time it happened in the middle of a class. I had had the feeling that something was going to happen, and had stayed close.

He must have listened to what I said. He had filled in the background. Karin Ærø handed him the drawing. A star had been stuck to the bottom left-hand corner. She said he had improved.

He took a step towards her.

"It's been coloured in," he said, "that's all."

I was right behind him. It was only two days since Flakkedam had stopped sitting behind us in class, and this was the first day he had not accompanied August up and down the stairs, or been in the playground at the intervals.

August and I had not talked about his situation, but even so we had an understanding. One evening, after I had paced round with him and just before he dropped off, he had asked about me, and I had told him how things stood: no parents, a scholarship, a guardian appointed and my case put before the Social Welfare committee of the local authority that had sent me for an indefinite period to Himmelbjerg House, and had it ratified by a judge.

"So that's why they let you into the cage," he said. "They've nothing special to lose."

While saying this he had slumped forwards and laid his head on his knees. And then he had smiled.

It was the first time I saw him smile. It made him seem so small.

Karin Ærø had stayed where she was when he moved towards her. She must have been warned, but maybe she thought he looked so harmless. And, one had to hand it to her, she never had been scared, no matter what. I had seen her hit Carsten Sutton before he was expelled. Hard, in the face, with a big paintbrush, out in the corridor, where there were other pupils and teachers.

August very nearly got to her. I grabbed his upper arms. They were skinny, but like steel. He shook as though he had a fever, but he was, in fact, cold.

I pulled him into the room where the pottery was put to dry. He stopped shaking and became much calmer than usual.

He had started waking me in the mornings. We had never talked about it, but he must have seen what a hard time I had waking up on those mornings when I had not slept at night. And then he had started sitting on my bed and shaking me, so that I could be sitting up before Flakkedam came.

Flakkedam woke you by the tube method. He started at your feet, chopping with the side of his hand, and worked his way up your body until you were on your feet. But now I was half up when he came, thanks to August.

Up to this point I had believed that the August who woke me in the morning was the only one. Now you could see that there was another. Facing up to Karin Ærø and when I grabbed hold of him

44

and pulled him away, he was someone else. There had to be two people living inside him, at the same time and yet taking it in turns. One could not help but think that, because of the other one – the one I had pulled away – both of them were lost.

9

OFTEN I DO NOT REACH the child. I watch her playing – it is a girl – I hear her calling. But I cannot reach her.

I am afraid that my own fear will be transmitted to her, that she will become every bit as scared as I am. So I thrust the woman between us, like a protective filter.

Can one protect a child from the world?

At any rate, one cannot teach it about the laboratory. Only those sucked into it can learn about the laboratory.

When the woman sings to the child one grows calm. Sometimes there are moments almost free of fear. I have been on the point of telling her; I have wanted to say it; have leaned over.

Karin Ærø sometimes leaned over, behind those who sang, on her way round the singers. And then she would say – quite softly, so that only the one to whom it was addressed should hear it:

"Excellent."

It is called praise. It is supposed to be a small act of kindness.

Next time she came past, and was right behind you, you could feel the fear from the one she had praised. Not a big fear, physical punishment did not enter into it. But a subtle, little fear that would perhaps only be obvious to someone who had never received much in the way of praise. The fear of not being just as good as last time; of not being worthy this time as well.

You knew that, always, when Karin Ærø came up behind you, so too came a judge.

Behind the woman I remembered Karin Ærø. So I said nothing.

*　　　*　　　*

To judge and assess. This was very important for the grand plan. Which was why you could not help but ask yourself whether Karin Ærø knew what she was doing. Did she know? That when one praises, one also judges. And then one does something that has a profound effect.

How much did they know? What did Biehl know?

The spoken word had been one of Grundtvig's principles. It meant that you were given very few books before Primary VI. Instead, the teachers recounted Danish history, Scandinavian history, world history, Greek and Norse mythology, Bible stories, the *Iliad* and the *Odyssey* to us – every day, five days a week.

It was a great many words. It called for the greatest awareness. Often, near the end of the day, it was impossible to remember anything except that someone had been talking at you.

Ever since I came to the school I had been looking for the rule behind the words, and at last I found it. It happened when August had been at the school for two weeks.

Biehl taught world history, he knew it by heart. Normally you kept quiet. Normally the spoken word was a stream that flowed down from the teacher's desk to the class. Until, suddenly, he asked a question. They came without warning – a handful of curt questions – and then it was very important that one could answer. When he asked a question it was as though, together with him, one closed in upon something crucial.

The questions always concerned an event and a date. Those on the inside could often remember them, those on the outside put their hands up out of fear, without remembering anything, and sank deeper into the darkness.

Personally, I had come close to giving up. I had tried to write down the dates he mentioned, but it was difficult, one could not know which ones would be the important ones, and taking notes in his classes was forbidden.

I would not have discovered it without Katarina. Even though we had not spoken to one another very often, and particularly not over the past few weeks. But she had been looking for something. When you meet a person who is searching you postpone giving up.

And then there was August. He had a lot of trouble remembering

47

things. During the first two weeks, not once had he been able to put up his hand. It seemed necessary to support him. If you want to support others you have to stay upright yourself.

I hit upon the rule by sensing Biehl. I had tried before, just after I came to the school, but with no luck. One could only observe him by letting go of time just a fraction; by stopping listening to what was being said and instead observing the voice and the face and the body. And then you ran a big risk. Then you took on a faraway look, and lost all sense of time and did not hear what was being said and could not be on the ball, just like that, if you were spoken to. That first time I had lost heart. Since then I had seen Katarina looking for something, so I gave it another try.

As Biehl approached the key points it was as though he became condensed. There was a brief pause. Then it came, without any special emphasis, almost casually. But condensed. Once I had felt my way to this, it was unmistakable. Then I understood.

The rule was: the Battle of Poitiers, 732.

At Poitiers the French king Charles Martel beat back the advancing Moors and thus saved Europe. A brilliant personage executed an appropriate deed at exactly the right moment. This was the pattern behind Biehl's questions. From then on I knew what I had to look for. Which of the overwhelming number of words one should remember. Columbus 1492, Luther at Worms 1521, Grundtvig's *Kirkens Gienmæle* in 1825 – in which it is established that truth is not based on books but on the spoken word from God's own lips at christenings and communions, expressed in the Apostles' Creed.

From then on I could, quite often, answer correctly. It gained me some time. It meant that it took longer for him to notice me.

· 10 ·

AFTER KATARINA had asked me about the car, I took to avoiding her; avoided even looking at her in the playground.

At the beginning of August's third week at the school she came up beside me on the stairs. Once she had passed, there was a letter in my pocket.

It was the first letter I had ever received. There had been others, but they had been printed.

It did not say who it was to, or who it was from. There was just a question: "Why were their children removed?"

A ban had been imposed on August – in the playground he was not to go any further away from the wall than that he could touch it with an outstretched arm. The first week, Flakkedam had walked on the outside of him, then the teacher on playground duty had taken over. Now it was no longer necessary, he kept to the wall by himself. No one said much to him either.

The only time he was allowed to leave it was to go to the toilet and then I had to go with him and wait outside until he was finished. That day I went in with him. There was barely room. We stood on either side of the toilet bowl while he smoked.

"I've had a letter," I said.

I showed it to him. He did not ask how I could be sure it was for me. He believed me. If I said it, it must be true.

Nor did he ask who it was from. He probably thought that would have been prying. All he said was: "What does she mean?"

*   *   *

In April 1971 all those pupils who were related to teachers were taken out of the school. Before that, Vera Hofstætter who taught German had had two boys in Primary II and Primary IV and Biehl had had two grandchildren in Primary I and Stuus who taught Latin had a daughter in third year Secondary and Jerlang had two children in Primary VIII and Primary VII and a girl, Anne, in our class. And then of course there was Fredhøj's son, Axel. Nine pupils altogether. They did not come back after the Easter holidays, nothing was said about it. Everyone reckoned it was because of what had happened to Axel Fredhøj.

Fredhøj was the deputy head, and well liked. His easy sense of humour made people open up, even those who had broken school rules. In this pleasant atmosphere they tended to give themselves away. After which Fredhøj was always ready with a remark – something good and quick – then the incident was forgotten. A couple of days later those who had forgotten themselves were summoned to Biehl's office, or their parents were summoned to an interview, or suddenly they were no longer in the class. They never saw what hit them.

Not once did I ever see him punish someone himself, all he did was pass the buck. It was brilliant.

It was hard if not impossible to see how Axel could be his son. You never saw them talking to one another, particularly not after the incident in the service corridors. Axel was in the class below us. Generally speaking you never heard him say a word except if a teacher asked him a question and even then only what was absolutely necessary.

Fredhøj taught physics and chemistry. He used a number of charts: the periodic table, Bohr's atomic theory, means of propulsion from the steam engine to the V6 engine, the major scientific developments. They were kept in the chart lockers – boxes of white-painted wood one and a half metres high, one and a half metres long and pretty narrow, with a puny furniture lock.

Fredhøj always went around with his keys in full view, hanging from the ring finger of his left hand on a good-sized key ring. The keys lay across the back of his hand. The keys to the chart lockers were on this ring.

It came out of the blue. It was a period no different from any other; the unfortunate incident in the service corridor lay six months back.

Fredhøj asked one of the bright girls, Anne-Dorthe Feldslev who was physics monitor, to fetch the periodic table. The class had its own ordinary monitor, who fetched the milk. It was something you took turns at, it was nothing special. But then there was a physics monitor who helped with the setting up of experiments and the like, whom Fredhøj selected from among the mathematically gifted. Just then it was Anne-Dorthe. She was not very strong and was let off gym, so at first you did not pay any attention. Fredhøj asked her to fetch the periodic table and gave her the keys. She went out into the corridor and opened the locker. Then she closed it again and came in and took her seat and put the keys down. Then she threw up. She did it all over the desk, where others might have tried to reach the washbasin or the wastepaper basket. But she never got up without permission.

Fredhøj must have realised that something was wrong. He stepped outside and lifted the lid. It was just outside the door.

In the locker sat Axel, looking up as though he had been waiting for someone to come and lift the lid. He had tried to cut out his tongue with a razor blade. He had got pretty far. The details did not come out until later, and then only some of them, but we saw the razor blade. Later on somebody said he had doped himself up beforehand.

What happened was that Fredhøj acted with assurance and precision, as with anyone else who hurt themselves, or needed first aid and an ambulance at once. Only our class was sent home, and as early as the next day it was announced at Assembly that Axel was out of danger.

We never saw him again. There was no inquiry of any description, it was never mentioned again. But everybody knew, three weeks later, when it was Easter and the teachers' children did not come back to school after the holidays, that this was the reason. It was perfectly obvious.

I told August about this, in the toilets, to explain the letter.

"If it was so obvious," he said, "then why is she asking?"

*   *   *

He was a head shorter than me, besides which he was always hunched up, like now. All hunched up, he looked up at me, across the toilet. He smoked a little bit at a time, then he put out the cigarette by very carefully pinching the tip and removing it, so as not to waste any tobacco. A little while later, he lit it again.

He smoked the way you only ever saw grown-ups smoke, and then only very seldom. Hungrily. It was a weird sight. The tiny body, and the hunger.

He was two years younger than me, one year younger than all the others in the class, because I had been put down a class when I came from Crusty House. They had never said where he came from. It was clear that he had trouble keeping up, even though he caught on fast. Even so, they had moved him up a class.

There was no chance to answer him. The door outside was opened, slowly, as if by a teacher. We had been in there a while and maybe we had been missed. We brushed away every speck of ash, flushed and left the toilets.

That evening he asked for an extra Mogadon but was met by a refusal.

He said nothing and only walked around for a short while, then he lay down as though he were sleeping.

It was not convincing.

Even so I almost did not hear him. We had been lying there for an hour – I could see by the alarm clock – then the door opened. Not that you could hear anything, but you felt the draught. He had moved very softly.

The exit was left unlocked at night. He made his way along the corridor to the basement stairs. The kitchen was in the basement. I thought he must be hungry, in which case he need not have bothered. There were padlocks on the fridges and freezers.

But that was not it. He did not switch on the light. It was as though he could see in the dark, like an animal. I stood at the top of the stairs. First there was silence, then the oven was opened. Then I went down after him and switched on the light.

He had opened the oven door, and stepped up on to it. He looked as though he were asleep, with the side of his head resting on the grille over the cooker top. He supported himself with one hand, gripped the knob with the other. He had closed his eyes. At first he did not notice the light. While I stood there, watching, he turned on the gas, just a little, and sort of drank from the tap. Then he shut it off again.

He opened his eyes and looked at me.

"I couldn't reach," he said.

"It's an industrial cooker," I said. "It's half a metre taller than the domestic ones."

His legs would not carry him. I gave him a piggyback. He was so light, even going up the stairs. There was a smell of gas from his mouth.

I put him down on his bed.

"I've got it taped," he said. "I sleep in the living room. When they've fallen asleep I go into the kitchen. You just have to have enough to get to sleep. But not so much that you can't get back to bed."

For some time the child has been talking about the space around her. She uses words like "outside" and "inside", "in" and "underneath". She goes into detail about her surroundings. She is twenty months old.

But not about time. As yet, "tomorrow", "yesterday", "in a month's time" hold no meaning for her. She says "some day", by which she means all forms of future.

We grasp the idea of space before we grasp that of time.

But soon she will begin to talk about time. And then she will say of it, that it passes.

We say that time passes. That it flies. That it is like a river. We picture it as having a direction and a length; that it can described in the same way as space.

But time is not space, is it? What I am doing now, in the laboratory, I also did yesterday. The two events belong in the same place, they are not separated in space. But they occupy different times.

And there is another difference. Thinking in terms of space is something one can do just like that. But thinking about time always carries pain in its wake.

Maybe it is the other way round; maybe the pain is there first. Because that is something one will always try to explain away.

Unaccountable pain overwhelms. So one tries to explain it away by means of time. That was what one had to say to oneself when one sat on the bed and August smelled as though he were full of gas. One had to say to oneself that it was because it was hard for him to fall asleep. That in itself was not disturbing; it was just a difficult time of the day for him. Time was the problem, one said to oneself.

As though that explained it.

Sometimes the child comes to see me, even though I am shut away in the laboratory. That is as it should be. It is part of an arrangement we have come to. Sometimes she talks to me; sometimes she says nothing, just comes close, hesitantly, aware, without aversion.

Sometimes she touches me. She puts out a hand, or leans against me. It is not a caress, like you see grown-ups exchanging. It is more as though, also through her sense of touch, she wants to confirm that I exist. Or as though she has a message for me.

I stayed by August's bed until he fell asleep. I hunkered down so that it would not feel as though I were crowding him.

It took him a while to drop off; even now it took a while. As though part of him needed to sleep, while another part was too scared to give in.

His hands lay on the duvet. They were clenched tight. Then I had an idea. I lifted one hand and opened it out, and then closed it over mine. He had tiny hands, so I closed it round three of my fingers. That way I would be able to tell when he fell asleep. His hand would fall open.

Like a message.

$$\left(\begin{array}{c} 11 \end{array}\right)$$

AT CRUSTY HOUSE if you had any personal problems you were supposed to consult your class teacher. That was Willy Øhrskov, who was popular and respected. He had a red MG and drove like a madman. When I had been there for six months he was killed in a car crash. And besides, talking about yourself to a teacher had always been considered a bit wet.

A consultant psychologist had been assigned to Biehl's, an elderly man with whom I had two sessions. He had difficulty in remembering my name. After the second one he said that, on the whole, everything seemed to be in order. After that I never saw him again.

Nine months went by. Then I received word that from now on I would have a standing appointment once a fortnight, during school hours, preferably in a handicrafts or storytelling period. You were fetched by one of the teachers, who let you out on to the south stairway – which was out of bounds. Then the door was locked behind you and you ascended to the fourth floor, and then further up a narrower stairway, to the school psychologist's clinic.

And there was Hessen.

The first time she asked me if I often thought about Humlum.

"Do you often think about Oscar?" she said.

Normally people only remembered your name, and often not even that. Hessen talked about Himmelbjerg House and the Royal

Orphanage and the time the judge ratified an indefinite period at approved school, and Humlum, as if we had met before.

And I came close to telling her everything. But I decided to wait.

Normally you did not talk to her about where all this was supposed to lead. You talked about other things, and you did some tests – Rorschach, projected perception tests and lots of IQ tests.

There was nothing in the room except a table and some chairs. Nothing ever lay on the table in front of her, not so much as a pencil. And yet she was always prepared, and could remember years and dates. Better than you remembered them yourself.

Together, every quarter, you took stock. You compared your own impressions with hers and the school's, and whatever supplementary information was to hand.

This was where I began to understand her.

It was her questions that gave the show away. They were so precise. In all the time I was referred to her she only committed one inaccuracy, and that was when she mentioned Katarina. Apart from that she was completely flawless.

I wondered about how she could know all the things she knew. Finally there was only one possible explanation. She must have had all of the papers, that was it, she was the first person I had met who was in possession of almost all the facts. The counsellor at Crusty House had known a fair bit, and one's class teacher Willy Øhrskov had known a fair bit, before his car crash, and at the office especially they had a lot of papers. But nowhere had they had all of them gathered together.

Hessen had all the statements and all the marks and all of the bad-conduct reports from the time at Crusty House. Besides which, she had the file – not just the ordinary one, but also the supplements from the child-psychiatry clinic at the University Hospital, which I had never seen. Not to mention the district medical officer's remarks and those from the dental clinic at Nyboder School. Also most of the documents from the Children's Panel, and a list of all the times

I had been late, when I had been monitor, and what chores I had been given, and whether I had given satisfaction.

In time it became clear that she also knew something about those times when I had been brought in for questioning. To begin with I could not figure this out. If you were under fifteen you could not have a criminal record. This was a rule. So I could not understand how she knew about that. Back then I could not figure it out, she just knew.

A vast amount of information. In many ways she knew more than you did yourself.

She was the first to realise that I had difficulties with time.

It was when we were taking stock after the third quarter. She must have added up all the times I had been late, or not handed things in on time. She had seen what Flage Biehl had written on my report card, namely that I did my best but had difficulty in concentrating and organising my time. And then she had our test results.

She told me that there were people who were born fast, and people who were not so fast, but that there was no point in being unduly slow, what could we do about that? We agreed that I would try to pull myself together. After that she brought it up every time.

When I visited her at the end of October, after August had been at the school for three weeks, I expected her to refer to my lack of precision again. Granted, only I knew how bad things were, but there had been no sign of improvement.

She did not mention it. She asked about August. Whether he lay awake at night, whether there were difficulties in sharing a room with him, whether he talked about his parents, to all of which I could reply in the negative.

She was very aware. I tried to work out what she was getting at, but she gave nothing away.

Then she said: "You know Katarina from second year Secondary?"

The question was wrongly posed. It was her first-ever inaccuracy.

*　　　*　　　*

57

I had worked out the rule behind her questions long before. She began by enquiring about my growing pains or my general state of health, or whether there was anything that had happened since last time that I would like to tell her about. Questions, the answers to which were already known and which were put simply to get me to say something, which I always did, although never very much. After that came the questions about my past and what I dreamed about at night.

When she mentioned Katarina it was different. It was a trap, the first one she had set for me.

She must have known that Katarina and I had been found together during a period. But she asked anyway. To see whether I would reply in the negative.

"We met at the library," I said. "Twice."

She asked me what we had talked about. Then I told an untruth.

There was no harm intended, but she had set a trap. One was forced into it.

"She said she would tell you herself when she comes up here."

There was a brief pause before she answered.

"She has not done so."

Thereby betraying the fact that Katarina had been up there, that she too had been referred to the psychologist. And that she had not told her anything special about us.

Then she asked how the conversation had come about. I knew I would have to answer.

"It was me," I said. "I wanted to find out what it was like to be alone with a girl."

It was not untrue. And you could see that it satisfied her. This was a rule I had discovered about her. Confessing to minor violations could lead to a reward of a sort.

AT LARS OLSEN'S MEMORIAL HOME they had a book – I borrowed it from the consultant – all about great clocks through the ages.

In China, before Christ, a clock consisted of concentric circles of incense through which a glowing ember burned its way, thus keeping pace with the day by way of constantly-changing scents.

At the same time, in Egypt, there was a grid – one hundred and fifty metres long, etched into rock – over which the shadow of an obelisk travelled with the sun.

In Europe, in the Middle Ages, there was a brass disc marked with a hypothetical stereographic projection of the heavens across which moved a mechanical model of the celestial bodies in bronze and wood. It was known as an astrolabe and called to mind another of the clocks in the book – the Chinese Sung dynasty's celestial clock: a model of the solar system mounted on a tower ten metres high and powered by a waterwheel as it presented the positions of the planets; the movements of the heavens; the months, days, hours and quarters.

The book had pictures.

It seemed so obvious then. That such precise clocks had always been regarded as technical marvels, more than anything else. They had not so much served another end – such as telling the time. They had been an end in themselves.

At the end of the fourteenth century many major European cities acquired a town clock.

In 1370, for example, the French duke Jean de Berry paid seventy per cent of the building costs on a very grand clock tower for Poitiers. Where Charles Martel had stopped the Moors.

This may well have been the first instance, anywhere in the world, of a timepiece which registered the passage of the hours being accessible to the general public.

But even then it was as though the time that the clock measured was not put to any use. For by far the majority of Europe's population, namely those living outside of the towns – and, strictly speaking, also for those living in them – the day began at dawn and ended with the onset of darkness, and work was regulated by the changing of the seasons.

What fascinated people about the measurement of time was not time itself, because that was dictated by other factors. What fascinated them was the clock.

The regularity of the clock was a metaphor for the accuracy of the universe. For the accuracy of God's creative achievement. So the clock was, first and foremost, a metaphor.

Like a work of art. And that is how it was. The clock has been like a work of art, a product of the laboratory, a question.

And then, at some point, this has changed. At some point the clock has stopped being a question. Instead it has become the answer.

At Biehl's, in every corridor, there hung a bell. That way, when the main bell went, it could be heard just as clearly all over the school.

The bell hung inside the corridor door, so high up that reaching it was out of the question, but still in full view.

Out of a black box containing an electro-magnet jutted a little clapper to strike the bell.

The bell was chrome-plated and polished regularly by the janitor, Andersen, who was referred to as Lemmy when out of earshot. It bore some sort of decoration, a pattern. It was too far away to make out the details, but you supposed that it must be in keeping with the school's overall decorative theme. It could have been a meander border or an entwining motif from one of the runic stones.

The bells looked as though they dated from the turn of the

century. Like Biehl's fob watch. Together they saturated the school with a finely-meshed web of time.

In the spring of '71 the bells were removed. Instead, a loudspeaker was set into the wall of each class. Behind the teacher's desk, beside the blackboard. A ringing tone was now transmitted over this; lower than the old mechanical one but, nevertheless, quite clear.

Furthermore, through this loudspeaker messages could be passed to a particular class from a central microphone in the headmaster's office, and you could answer by speaking in the direction of the loudspeakers.

And it turned out that, from the office, a line could be opened in such a way that Biehl could hear what was going on in the classrooms, without you knowing it. In this way they could make sure that order reigned even if, for example, a class had to wait a few minutes for a teacher.

The loudspeaker sat behind a white panel, so that it was, to all intents and purposes, invisible.

The old bells had been regularly polished. The new were invisible. We did not see them being delivered, nor the old ones being removed. We came back to school and the job was done.

They had done it during the Easter holidays. The same Easter that the teachers' children were removed.

13

AFTER SUPPER – from 19.00 to 20.15 – there was compulsory prep for boarders in the main hall, supervised by Flakkedam. During this time there was a ban on leaving the hall. It was difficult for August. Even during the day he had trouble sitting still, but in the evening it got worse, as the time for his medicine approached.

I sensed that it was very bad, so I went to see Flakkedam in the duty room and asked permission for August and me to go outside for a minute. To decline the irregular German verbs together, without disturbing the others. I explained that, you know, he had been moved up a class, so he had not had German before. Permission was granted.

It was dark. You could sense that he felt better outside, but not much. Here, too, he looked for the walls. He would not walk along the paths or across the grass, but made for the fringes of the shrubbery.

We walked for a bit side by side. He walked along looking up at me.

"What's it like in a children's home?" he said.

"Okay," I said.

"How do you survive?"

"You just do," I said, "no problem, and can we get back to the hall now, time's up."

"Not yet," he said. "First you have to answer; I don't want to go inside."

We carried on. He walked slowly, he listened. For the first time since we had met.

"You have to have a strategy," I said.

He shivered as he walked. He had come out without a jacket. I took off my sweater and pulled it over his head, the way you dress a child. If he caught a cold they would ask why I had not looked after him. He put up no resistance. His arms did not go into the sleeves. They just hung there, dangling.

"I had a friend who ate frogs," I said. "He was dangerous as well, but that wasn't the main thing. If you're alone it doesn't matter how dangerous you are. The main thing was the frogs. The grown-ups knew about them too. It's hard to touch someone you've seen eat a frog. That was his strategy."

I did not expect him to understand.

"If you can't remember anything," he said, "if the light in your brain has simply been put out, that would be a pretty good strategy, eh?"

So he had, after all, understood.

We walked back to the annexe.

"Why does she ask?" he said. "Why does she write, asking why the teachers' children were removed?"

It was early to tell him about it, but we were walking together. For the first time we were walking side by side and at absolutely the same pace. So I told him.

It took a month. That was what was so strange. From the time when Axel was found in the chart locker until the children related to teachers were removed – it took a month. An inexplicable pause between the catastrophe and its consequences.

It was then, too, that the loudspeakers were installed in the class-rooms, and when one was allocated a standing appointment with the psychologist once a fortnight, and when one saw Hessen for the first time, and her two assistants, and then there were other things too. Somehow, all of this seemed too much to be because of Axel.

"What sort of other things?" he said.

It was Flakkedam. It was at that time that they had appointed Flakkedam.

Before that, at Biehl's, and at the Orphanage, and at Himmelbjerg

House, the boarders had always been supervised by a teacher. In other words, it was he who checked that chores were done and sat with the pupils in the dining room and supervised prep and put out the lights at 22.00 hours. There might well be others who assisted him, but the person in charge had always been a qualified teacher – it was a rule.

Flakkedam was not a teacher.

At the Orphanage and at Himmelbjerg House there had also been staff who were not teachers. At the bottom, under the matron and the deputy and the department heads and the teachers and the senior assistants and the social workers there had been auxiliaries or porters. These had been gardeners' labourers, or NCOs or former accountants who, for one reason or another, had not been able to cope in their previous place.

It was different with Flakkedam.

You never saw him drink alcohol, you never saw him hit anyone, never, not once. He just had to appear on the scene and people grew absolutely quiet, out of fear.

In the corridors he walked only a little bit in front of Biehl. In the yearbook for '71 it said that, in April, the school had bidden welcome to Superintendent Jonas Flakkedam.

"Superintendent." No further explanation.

"He stands on my foot," said August. "When he's checking that I take the medicine, he stands on my foot. I can't move. He's good."

64

I FELL ASLEEP that night, but I must have heard him in my sleep. When I checked, he was gone.

He was finished by the time I got there. He stood polishing the cooker with his sleeve. The light was on. He was swaying.

I got him on to my back. From up there he talked to me.

"There was never any washing-up," he said.

I told him to be quiet, Flakkedam would hear him.

"The fingermarks had to be wiped off," he said, "she would have spotted them right away."

I put him down on the bed.

"There must be another way," I said, "something other than gas."

His eyes were half-open, but he was sleeping. I closed his fingers round my hand.

"She always looked like a million dollars," he said.

After a while his hand fell open, but he was restless. So I shook him gently. That calmed him down a bit.

The thought came to me that, if you ever had a child, it might be like that. It was inconceivable that such a thing could happen, but still, if it did.

Then you would watch over it. If it were restless you would not sleep at night. I would cope without sleep. I would sit by its side and, now and again, when it moved and sighed restlessly, like August, you would stretch out a hand and shake it.

There would be nothing personal in it. But if I were assigned responsibility for a child, I would keep watch.

The room smelled of gas. The thought came to me that August

was probably lost. This thought grew as the night went on and finally became too much to cope with. Around midnight I decided to talk to Katarina about it.

The girls' wing was separated from the boys' by a glass door fitted with an alarm that was activated by a sliding contact with connectors. The duty room, where Flakkedam slept, was just above this. I could have deactivated the alarm, but only if I had had tools.

Instead I jumped from the window of the janitor's store room. I had a blanket with me, and a wire coat hanger and a cardboard folder stuck to my stomach with a plaster.

Not long after Flakkedam came to the school, and in connection with the renovations, various things had been done to make the annexe more homely. At this juncture, a rose bed had been laid out. No one thought twice about it. Flakkedam had a thing about flowers. He had chosen potted plants personally, and supplied all the posters that were used to brighten up the inside. Most of those had had something to do with flowers – a healthy and a sick tulip, that was a warning against drug abuse.

The bed was raked over every afternoon, between the roses too. It was one of the set chores. One morning, when I had been sitting looking out of the window, and had not slept at night, I saw Flakkedam. It was very early. He walked the length of the rose bed, looking at the soil. If there had been footprints he would have seen them immediately.

The bed was three metres wide, and ran right up against the house. It was difficult, if not impossible, to jump from a window without leaving a print in the soil, which was, of course, always freshly-raked. It was a brilliant set-up.

So it was necessary to jump from the store-room window. From there you could jump at an angle on to the stairs leading up to the entrance. It was not the easiest place to land, but it was the only choice. The main door was locked.

* * *

It was cold and very clear. There were only a few leaves on the trees, you could see stars and the lights of Copenhagen.

At Himmelbjerg House there had been a plan for when you were to run away. It was strictly regulated: two at a time, with a fortnight between. You took a car and saw who could get furthest away and stay out the longest. This was to put pressure on the grown-ups, but also so you could bum around in freedom.

The first few hours after you had left the building, when it was night, had always felt good. Even after I realised that it would, in the long run, lead to perdition and had stopped, and then had trouble with the others and started working on being transferred to Crusty House – even then I had missed it. The feeling of it being night; of the teacher on duty being asleep; of the world being spread at your feet; of anything being possible, freedom – absolutely brilliant.

Now it was different. The feeling was there, but it was different. Somewhere above and behind me August lay sleeping. That made a difference. You knew he was lying there, tossing and turning. It was as though a clock had started ticking as I left him, and now the countdown had begun.

You started wondering how people could ever abandon their children. How can you abandon a child?

I climbed up the drainpipe. There was no risk, the outside of the building had been repaired at the same time as the rose bed was made and the renovations done.

Also at that time, they had installed double glazing, but only the standard windows, with a lever that did not lock, just closed over the other window. I opened it with the coat hanger.

I sat for a moment on the windowsill, feeling my way. Three breathing.

Beneath the window slept the girl with whom she shared the room. She was familiar, she was one of the diplomatic children whose father was an ambassador and abroad somewhere. In the dark Katarina was asleep. Behind her breathing there was another's.

It was Flakkedam's – deep, quite peaceful and penetrating. He had to be in the next room, just on the other side of the wall.

I pulled the window shut, but without closing it to with the lever.

Then I climbed across the diplomatic girl and made my way over to Katarina.

I stood by her bedside for a moment.

Sometimes, at Høve, at the rest home for underprivileged children, you crept into the girls' dormitory at night, and stood alone in the dark and felt their presence.

But there had been eighty girls there. That had been almost too much. This was different.

I stretched out an arm and shook her gently. She woke up. As she drew breath to scream I put a hand over her mouth and cut off the sound. "It's me," I said. She sat up, but I did not let go of her until she calmed down.

"I've come about August," I said.

It was necessary to whisper, very softly, lips right up against her ear. She did not pull away.

"There's a plan behind the school," I said; "August won't be able to cope with it. The idea is that time raises up."

Until that moment I had held this back from everyone else, even from her. Now I had to trust.

"If you went blind," I said. "If you were used to finding your way around a house and then, suddenly, one day had an accident – were attacked or something – and became blind, only then would you actually notice the furniture. It would always have been there, but you would never have been aware of it, you would just have gone round it. Only when something becomes hard to cope with do you see it. That's how you become aware of time – when it becomes hard to cope with."

Her hair was in the way. I brushed it back and sat holding it for a moment, so it would not fall back. I was resting against the place in the bed where she had been lying. It was still warm. I knew what I wanted to say, I had gone over it in my head beforehand.

"If you can manage to stay on at the school – if you have committed no serious violations or acts of gross negligence – then you're here for ten years. During those ten years your time will be strictly regulated, there will only be very few occasions when you are in doubt as to where you should be or what you should be doing, very few hours altogether where you have to decide anything for yourself. The rest of the time will be strictly regulated. The bell rings – you go up to the classroom, it rings – you come down, it rings – you eat, rings – work, rings – eat, rings – prep, rings – three free hours, rings – bedtime. It's as if there are these very narrow tunnels that have been laid out and you walk along them and nowhere else. They're invisible, like glass that has just been polished. You don't see it if you don't fly into it. But if you become blind or short-sighted, then you have to try to understand the system. I've been trying for a long time. Now I know."

The other girl felt so close, Flakkedam was just on the other side, their breathing was right beside us the whole time. We were talking in a little space between two breaths or, in fact, between three because somewhere beneath us August lay, breathing restlessly. You could not hear it, but even so, to me he was there.

She drew the duvet over our heads, to muffle our voices. There we sat, as though in a tent or a sleeping bag. I gave nothing away. I kept going so that she would understand me.

"There is a selection that takes place. People are selected according to the laws of nature. The school is an instrument dedicated to elevation. It works like this. If you achieve in the way you're supposed to, time raises you up. That's why the classrooms are arranged as they are. From Primary I to III you're on the ground floor, then you move up to the first floor, then the second, then to Secondary on the third, until at last – at the very top, in the assembly hall – you receive your certificate from Biehl. And then you can fly out into the world."

There, I had said it. We were nearing the conclusion.

"I've been wondering why it is so hard for them, why there are so many rules. And it occurred to me that it is because they have to keep the outside world out. Because out there it's not everywhere that it raises up. There are lots of places out there where time drags you downwards towards destruction. That is what they must keep out. You must be left in no doubt that the world raises you up, otherwise it would be impossible to cope with the expectations. Coping is something you do best when you believe in time. If you believe that the whole world is an instrument through which you become elevated, just so long as you do your best – that is the metaphor the school presents. It's brilliant."

She moved her face until her lips were close beside my ear.

"What about you?" she said.

Her voice was husky with sleep. Well, I had woken her up.

It was not absolutely clear what it was she was asking, but I answered anyway.

I said that, as far as I was concerned, special circumstances came into play; since I was ill but at the same time had a personal insight into my illness – according to my record. I brought it out. That was what I had had stuck to my stomach. If she felt like it, she could read it. It was the bit I had been given a copy of at Nøde-bogård remand home. So it was not complete. You did not get to see the confidential bit, but even so it was enlightening. This made it quite clear, I said, that if you were to have any chance after having grown up in a children's home, there had to have been one particular grown-up to whom you had formed an attachment. In my case, there had not been. For various reasons, within the first ten years of my life, I had been in four different institutions. So I was damaged. It said so, in so many words – that it was difficult, if not impossible, for me to establish stable emotional relationships – in other words, to have any deep feelings. There was nothing personal in my coming here tonight. She could tell that from the record. I had come because of August.

"He sniffs gas," I said.

That is not what I meant to say. I meant to say that he was like a wild animal that has been cooped up; a bird of prey, that keeps flying into the invisible, polished glass, but I could not get it out, I had done too much talking. Even so, it was as if she had understood.

"He drinks from the gas tap in the kitchen to be able to sleep," I said. "He doesn't fit in at the school, he'll never be able to cope with it. What can be done?"

She did not answer me. Nor had I expected an answer. It was not clear what it was I was asking. There was August, back in our room, I had to leave. And I was very close to her.

She caught up with me halfway across the floor.

"There's something I don't understand," she said.

She was right behind me, she had forgotten herself and had spoken out loud.

"He is chaos," she said. "If their plan is order, why have they taken him?"

*   *   *

70

Order.

When the child was about a year old she started talking. At first it was just single words, but pretty soon they formed into strings. Into lists.

She would come and sit close beside me. You had the feeling that there was something she wanted to explain. I said nothing.

Then she would start reciting all the words she knew. First the objects around us but, after that, things she had seen and heard the names of, some of them just the once.

Very rarely did she ask a question. It was rather as though there was something she wanted to say; that something being these long lists.

They took two forms. In the afternoon it was objects, in the evening people. Before she went to sleep, before the woman came in to her, I would sometimes sit on her bed. She lay on her back, she would be close to dropping off. Then she would start to name the names of all the people she knew, or whom she had met, or of whom she had only heard – a very great number of names.

She could go on for long enough, perhaps as much as half an hour. It was impossible to understand how one child could contain so many people.

From the start I knew that, in what she was saying, there lay a message.

The first thing one realised was that she did it all of her own accord. There was no external prompt, no encouragement or reward. It was the first thing one noticed.

There had to be pleasure simply in using the words. It was the first time I understood this. That, if no one hinders a person, or assesses them, then maybe there is pleasure in just being allowed to use the words.

There is no explanation for this pleasure. It is like the questions in the laboratory – that is to say, uncertain and impossible to put more clearly.

Apart from this pleasure there was yet another, profound, message. I understood this the first time I was left alone with her.

The woman had gone out. Just as she was leaving, she looked at me for a moment and I knew that perhaps she was doing this – I mean, leaving us alone – for my sake.

The child sat beside me on the sofa. I looked at her and the thought occurred to me that now this was my responsibility. For the first time.

I had looked after people before; looked after some of the ones you went to school with. That had been easier. They had been a bit older, and most of them were having a pretty bad time of it. You had known that no matter what you did, things could not get much worse for them. Even with August it had been simpler. All you could do for him was try to find the last resort.

With the child it is different. You have this idea that maybe there is a chance for her. That no one has ruined anything for her yet. That she can eat what she wants and she has the woman and is with a family, and she has never been hit.

Then comes a time when you are alone with her, and then it is difficult to know what you are supposed to do.

You know that the only thing in her life that means anything is the woman, and she has gone out. The only one left is you. Who are pretty much useless. And who has nothing special to give to other people.

It was unnerving, you have no idea what you are supposed to do. I grew pretty uneasy.

To begin with I said nothing, did nothing.

She had walked over to the door through which the woman had left. She called to me from there. I went over to her.

She was very grave. The skin of her face seemed very thin, ready to split, like paper. Beneath it lay an unfathomable sorrow.

But she did not cry. It was as though she were trying out something.

"We wait here," she said.

We sat down, with our backs against the door. The hallway was cold. We sat side by side. Then she looked up at me.

"Mummy back soon," she said.

Soon. It was the first time she had ever referred to time.

Then I understood the message in her lists.

It was order. The message was order. What she had told me was that she was trying to put the world in order.

72

On the floor, when I had sat down beside her, I had seen, as if through her eyes, how the world seemed to her. Big. Overwhelming. Through this chaos, by way of the words, she tried to lay tunnels of order.

To organise is to recognise. To know that, in an endless, unknown sea, there is an island upon which you have set foot before. It was islands such as these that she had been pointing out. With the words she had created for herself a web of familiar people and objects.

"Mummy back soon."

She had introduced order into the chaotic sorrow at being separated from the woman by explaining that there was a time limit, that this was temporary, that it would come to an end. She had used time in order to cope with the pain of separation.

Around a child, people come and go, objects appear and are taken away, surroundings take shape and disintegrate. And no explanation is given, because how can you explain the world to a child?

So she had used the words. Words summon up and secure that which has gone away. With her lists she had ensured that whatever she had once known would come back.

She looked up at me. Her eyes were full of tears, but she was not crying, it was as though she were coping with the sorrow.

Wordlessly her face told me that we belonged together. That we both knew something about loss. Even she – who had so much more than I had ever had – even she already knew that this was a world where people and things were taken away from you; where you are shifted from where you want to be; where someone switches off the light and you tumble into fear. There may be no hurt intended, but it is unavoidable.

I suppose that, up until that moment, I had not really understood that she was a person. I had thought of her, rather, as something especially precious that you could protect in the way that you had never been protected.

Now I saw that in a way she was like me. Much, much more pure and precious, but still, in a way, just like me.

Then the thought occurred that maybe I could be of benefit to her anyway, that I still might be able to reach her.

*   *   *

73

I do not know how long we sat there. It came to the point where she slowly curled up and went to sleep. I carried her to bed. I sat down and looked at her. I thought about what she had said, and why.

She had said it to overcome her sorrow at the woman's absence. But she had said it to me.

I waited in the grounds for several hours. It was very cold, even though I had the blanket. Flakkedam came before it was light, he let himself out of the entrance and left it open, then he started on his tour of the rose bed. When he had gone, I slipped inside. August was fast asleep. The window had been left open. The smell of gas was gone.

15

KATARINA LET three days go by after my visit. I knew she had not forgotten us or given up. I did not see her when she came. Suddenly she was just there, behind me, in the playground.

"Don't look round," she said.

I checked out the teacher on duty anyway.

"They're forgetting us," she said.

I had had the same thought. That was the way of the rule. They had so many to keep an eye on. As long as you kept a low profile, in time you would be forgotten. It was the best thing that could happen.

"You two have third period free," she said. "We can meet at the clinic."

The clinic was Hessen's clinic. Which was out of bounds and impossible to get at.

"It's Wednesday," she said. "The door on the ground floor will be open, they'll be bringing in the milk."

During free periods you could do homework or read a book of your choice, but you could not leave the class. I let fall a remark about having to go to the toilet, just in case the channel to the office was open. And August had to come with me, since I had been ordered never to leave him behind in the classroom.

Outside, I did not say where we were going, he would have refused. I just twisted his arm up his back, and marched him along. He put up no resistance.

The door to the south stairway was open. We ascended to the fifth floor without meeting a soul.

The clinic was not locked, it could not be locked. I had talked about this to Hessen – we talked openly about things like that, as part of my personal insight into my illness. When the clinic was set up, she had expressly requested that the lock be removed, so that no one would feel cooped up. She had said that this should be the place in the school where you felt most free and welcome.

I opened the door and went in. Katarina was sitting on a chair over by the window.

There was a big mirror on the wall, between the door to the next room and the loudspeaker panel. Hessen had told me that she had been an instructor in Mensendieck gymnastics. Now and again we had rounded off my visits to her by my having to take off my shirt and my vest. Then we would stand side by side facing the mirror and I had to move my arms and shoulders and head in different ways. She had explained that this could, in the long run, correct my bad posture. Now the mirror seemed like a hole, or like something, watching you. It had curtains. I drew them.

I took off my shoes and socks, removed the panel over the loud-speaker and laid the socks over the membrane. It was not one hundred per cent safe, but it would muffle the sound.

It would not have done to sit at the table where one had so often sat with Hessen. I took the chair over to the window and sat August on it. I remained standing.

He sat there, looking out of the window. It did not seem possible that she would ever get through to him. I had had three weeks, but no more than a few minutes of contact. The rest of the time he had been cooped up inside himself. Besides which, it was the first time they had met.

"There is a plan behind the school," she said. "So many things happen, you're never given any explanation. We are going to study it scientifically, like in a laboratory."

She did not look straight at him. She must have sensed that he could not bear that. Nor did she look at me, who, in fact, was not all that keen on it either. She looked at a point between us, she had spoken pretty softly. She unfolded two pieces of paper.

"This is the teachers' timetable," she said, "and Hessen's. I copied them out."

She spoke to August without looking directly at him.

"I was late five times. For that you get sent to Biehl. I came early on purpose and waited in the secretary's office. The timetable is

stuck up on the wall. When the secretary went out I copied it down
– as much I could manage. The rest I worked out by asking around
the other classes. Once I had it, I could draw up a plan of when
the rooms were in use. These two timetables, together with the
pupils' one that I had already constructed – they give the whole
schedule for the entire school. That's all I wanted to say. You can
go now if you don't want to be in on this."

At first he was quiet. Then he pulled up his shirt. He had some
papers tucked in against his stomach. He unfolded them. It was the
two drawings – the one that had found favour and the first one,
where the background had not been filled in. He did not throw his
drawings away like other people.

"You draw something," he said, "and you get nothing. Then you
do the same thing again, but this time you get a star and are praised,
how come?"

He said it casually, without looking at her. He was testing her.
If she got it wrong she would have lost him.

She looked at the drawings. It was as though she were listening
to them, in the same way that she had listened to me – then I knew
that she would reach him.

"It's something to do with time," she said. "You got a star
because you had spent more time on the second drawing. And spent
the time in a particular way. We think they have a plan, and that
it has to do with time."

"So the second one wasn't any better?"

Now that he was looking straight into her face, she was careful
not to meet his gaze.

"There's no such thing as better," she said. "The second one just
fitted in better with their plan."

How could she know that? She was only sixteen, how could she
know that and say it?

When is one thing better than another? It is a crucial question.

Although, usually, what one has in mind is that something is
not good enough. Oscar Humlum, for example, was just not good
enough. Axel Fredhøj did not think he was either. Nor I. It said in

77

the record: "of average intelligence", but right from the start they had acknowledged that that was probably stretching things a bit.

That, even so, it is I who am left, and able to ask questions, here, in the laboratory, and not Humlum, for example, is not because I was better – I have never said that. I just wanted so badly to live.

At Crusty House, in a four-hundred-metre race, it was always possible to determine who could run better than everyone else. And pretty often in football, you could say that one pass was better than another. But it was actually less common than you might imagine. And mainly in straightforward situations offering very few openings.

In Biehl's classes it was obvious when an answer was correct.

With Karin Ærø things were a little less clear-cut but, on the whole, there was never any serious doubt as to who sang true enough to be in the choir.

One has to be left with the impression that this thing about assessing the merit of a person's singing or answers or football was something straightforward, something strictly regulated.

But in all of these instances an answer did, already, exist. That you had to score, or remember a particular date or sing true or run a distance under a certain time. There was a clearly defined quadrangle of knowledge – like a chessboard, like a football pitch. So it was pretty easy to see what was correct and what was wrong, when one thing was better or worse than another. But if it became just a little bit more complicated, as at the opening of an attack, or in midfield, then you could no longer be sure what the answer would be. As with August's drawing. You would think, in that case, that it would have to be almost impossible – after all, it was his. How could an answer already exist as to how it should be?

When you assess something, you are forced to assume that a linear scale of values can be applied to it. Otherwise no assessment is possible. Every person who says of something that it is good or bad or a bit better than yesterday is declaring that a points system exists; that one can, in a reasonably clear and obvious fashion, set some sort of a number against an achievement.

But never at any time has a code of practice been laid down for the awarding of points. No offence intended to anyone. Never at any time in the history of the world has anyone – for anything ever so slightly more complicated than the straightforward play of a ball or a four-hundred-metre race – been able to come up with a code of practice that could be learned and followed by several different people, in such a way that they would all arrive at the same mark. Never at any time have they been able to agree on a method for determining when one drawing, one meal, one sentence, one insult, the picking of one lock, one blow, one patriotic song, one Danish essay, one playground, one frog or one interview is good or bad or better or worse than another.

Never at any time. Nothing that comes anywhere near a code of practice.

But a code of practice is essential. To ensure that things can be spoken of, fully and frankly. A code of practice is something that could be passed on, maybe not to a character like Jes Jessen, or me, but at any rate to someone like Katarina or a teacher.

But, in all the history of the world, no code of practice has ever existed for the assessment of complex phenomena.

And certainly not for what crops up in the laboratory.

And yet everyone talks in terms of what is good or bad. And now and again they can be pretty much in agreement. For example, everyone was pretty much in agreement that, in Oscar Humlum's case – the bit I have not been able to talk about yet – it was no great loss. Nor, in fact, in Axel Fredhøj's, and definitely Jes Jessen's. Apart maybe from me and a handful of others – we were not in agreement. The thing about Humlum, that did not go down very well with me – and not just because he had saved me, that had happened long before. Since then, not a day has gone by that I have not thought of him. It is over twenty years ago now. Often he is there, between one's dreaming and one's waking; often he comes to the laboratory and talks to me. For a long time after it happened it was enough to drive you insane. Sometimes, the way you felt, you wished you could go insane.

But that is not how it works, you cannot just go crazy. And then, when you have been selected to be average, or a bit below, you have to do something else in order to keep going. You have to develop a strategy.

I suppose that is why I have focused on the part about the assessments.

If no code of practice exists for determining when something is good or bad, why do people talk as though it does? How could they be so sure when they awarded stars and points and wrote notes in the record and decided who was gifted in mathematics or art and referred Humlum to the Central Mission Home for the Retarded on Gersonsvej, and committed me, for an indefinite period, to Himmelbjerg House because the fact that I was of average intelligence amounted to exacerbating circumstances? If there is no code of practice, why is everyone so very, very sure?

Katarina came close to an explanation.

That first time, at the clinic, she only mentioned the bit about the stars and time. But that was enough. For me, in a way, that has continued to be enough – for the whole of my life up to this point.

How could she know that they had never been able to prove that one thing is better than another?

She had probably not worked it out logically. Actually, I would have to say I believe that I gave more thought to it than she did. The greater the fear the more thinking you do. Yet she came closer to the truth than anyone else.

Maybe that is how it works – that whatever is closest to the truth, you do not think about; you cannot reach it by achievement; you can only feel it. And feeling, that is something you can do, even when you are only sixteen.

While she was talking about his drawings he had stood up.

"I knew there was a conspiracy," he said.

I sat him back on the chair.

"We have to get back soon," I said. "We're at the toilet."

He did not hear me.

"What about you, chummie?" he said. "Where do you fit into this?"

I knew what he meant. That she was, after all, one of the posh kids – she could not have problems. So what was in this for her? That was what he meant.

But she understood. That she had to give him something in return, if she wanted him to join us.

"You have this idea that it must be terrible when people hang themselves," she said, "that they fall a long way. But it doesn't have to be like that."

She spoke as though we knew what all this was about, and as though August knew the bit about her mother too. She said that, with her father, on the surface things had been quiet and calm. After her mother's death it was as though he began to dread the daylight, if you could imagine such a thing. Often he did not get up, and, when he did, he would just sit there waiting for the day to pass. Often he would sit and stare at a clock. As if trying to make the seconds pass more quickly. In the end he had gone off to their farmhouse in Sweden – where they used to go every summer – and there he hanged himself, in the sitting room.

"From a door handle," she said, "you don't have to do it from high up. He put a rope around his neck and then he sat down and put a bit of weight on the rope so that it tightened and stopped his circulation. Then he lost consciousness and all his weight pulled down on it, and he was dead.

"Once it's happened," she said, "you're left with it, so you have to do something."

"So why this thing about a laboratory?" asked August.

She started to sing. Just one verse. At first you thought she was going crazy. The words were familiar, we had sung them often at Assembly, but this time they sounded different.

". . . to the Christ child's crib my heart is ever brought
There I can gather the sum of all my thoughts."

She was in the choir, but even so it was incredible that she sang alone.

"That was where I got the idea," she said. "You have to have a place where you can gather your thoughts. Like people who pray. That is what is difficult here at the school. Peter says it is like glass tunnels. There is no chance to think for yourself. A laboratory is a place that is shut off, so you have peace and can think and carry out your experiment."

She had got to her feet and started walking back and forth.

"It is already under way. It is the middle of a period, we are not where the plan says we should be, we have stepped out of the glass tunnel. The experiment is already under way. Something is happening to us, can you feel it? What is it? What's happening is that you are starting to become restless, you want to get back, you can feel time passing. That feeling is your chance, you can feel your way and learn something you would otherwise never have seen. Like when I came late on purpose. I stepped out of the tunnel I was used to walking along, I saw Biehl, and I noticed something."

August was sitting bolt upright. He did not say a word, but his body was listening.

"He's scared too," she said.

"Why me?" said August.

She was standing over by the other door, beside the mirror. There was a lock on it, no one knew where it led. She answered in all honesty.

"We have to find out why they took you. There is no understanding it."

There was no harm intended. She just said exactly what she thought.

A sound came over the loudspeaker. I made a sign to the others, then I removed the socks. The sound was very faint, you could not tell anything from it except that the channel had been opened.

I put on the socks. Katarina put back the chairs, quite soundlessly. Then I went out on to the stairs and looked down.

They were on their way up from the second floor. I stepped back inside and closed the door. It was Fredhøj and Flakkedam, you could identify them by Fredhøj's jacket sleeve and Flakkedam's shirt. It could have been worse, Biehl himself could have been with them. He only came for serious accidents, like with Axel Fredhøj, or for on-the-spot expulsions.

Even so, I thought this was the end, at any rate for August and me. We had already gone way over the limit.

There was a knock at the door. They could just have opened it, but at Biehl's one always knocked first. High up in the doors to the infant classes there were small panes of glass. Before the loud-speaker system was installed Biehl used to do his rounds of the new teachers, peeking in through the glass to see whether they could control the pupils. If there was any trouble, he came in. But even then he had knocked first.

Katarina was about to say something, she did not get the chance. They opened the door.

Normally they separated people for a certain length of time – one or two months for example – but in our case there were special, exacerbating circumstances.

We were questioned individually, and then we were isolated from one another, for an indefinite period. Each of us was assigned to our own part of the playground. They moved August out of my room and back to the sickbay. We still sat together in class, though, because there was no opportunity for conversation during periods.

It was Fredhøj who examined us. He told me that he had been requested to present me with my final warning.

II

TIME?

Soon I must say. But not yet. It is still too early.

Biehl's podium was wooden, with Greek columns. On it were carved the words "I and my house shall serve the Lord", and further down, "Under the shadow of Thy wings".

So, protection and darkness. As a hen gathers her chicks under her wings. As if to protect them from birds of prey.

Above the inscription stood the school crest. The ever-watchful ravens.

The ravens seemed to be looking down upon the inscription. As though they were the birds of prey, gazing down upon the chicks.

At first you understood neither text nor image. Then it was explained to you and for a while you thought you understood it.

Then the thought occurred that the school seemed to be both the protective hen – God, that is – and the birds of prey – the ravens; God's messengers; who preyed on the chicks.

You ended up understanding none of it.

Behind the podium, and therefore above and behind Biehl when he was speaking, hung a large painting of Delling, the god who unlocks the gates of morning. A young man opens a great gate, and out across the podium and into the hall springs a white horse, Skinfakse – the steed of Light. The painting also shows a black horse, Rimfakse – Night – moving out of the picture.

Biehl explained all of this. It was a metaphor, both of Assembly and of enlightenment and knowledge.

87

The man, Delling, in the picture was slightly built, like a child. Actually, he looked just like August. Not to make a big thing of it; there was no way it could be a painting of him, after all it was from the last century. It is just that, after we became separated, it struck me that it looked like him.

So: the door is opened and knowledge washes over you, like sunlight. That was the explanation that was given. Meaning that enlightenment is something that already exists. The only achievement necessary from your side is that of being open to it.

At Biehl's Academy natural science was seen as the supreme branch of learning. The same was true of the Royal Orphanage and, in fact, as far back as Himmelbjerg House, the mathematically gifted were considered to have the highest level of intelligence.

Biehl himself had an MSc in biology. Fredhøj taught mathematics and physics.

It was not that the other subjects were not worthwhile. Biehl also taught history and mythology.

But natural science ranked above all.

This tied in with the fact that it was not subject to human uncertainty.

The other subjects – even written and oral interpretation, for which there were strict rules – even these were subject to a degree of uncertainty. Even Diderichsen's grammatical tables did not hold good one hundred per cent of the time.

But with the periodic table there were no exceptions. Step by step you ascended, from the simplest, base elements to the precious and complex and rare. Like climbing a stairway; each step corresponded to an established increase in the atomic weight, and another element.

It was never said in so many words. But you could not help thinking that it resembled the evolution of the species. The ascent from simple, primitive organisms to the complex and highly developed.

It was never said in so many words. But that is how things were arranged on the charts. An outline of the evolutionary process resembled the periodic table. At the bottom: oxygen, hydrogen and amoebae. At the top: gold and mankind. And between them ran the links, like steps on a stairway.

Alongside and up through this stairway flowed time. The final elements in the periodic table were to be found only in the laboratory, produced by man. Whom it had taken evolution all this time to produce.

As a rule, in physics and mathematics, you were working with things far removed from yourself. Because they were very big or very small. Like atomic weights or the great astronomical discoveries. Now and again, though, science could get very close to you. As with the covert Darwinism, and the golden mean of violence and the law concerning the guiding importance of the beginning.

Regarding the great scientific discoveries, Fredhøj had told us that these had been made by great mathematics and physics geniuses who had not yet turned thirty. It was something he returned to again and again. His favourite example was Einstein who was twenty-five when he published his theory of relativity; when he had his *annus mirabilis* in 1905. Fredhøj said, if you are to achieve anything in your life, you have to do it before you turn thirty.

When he said that you could not help but think of his own son, Axel. That, if he were to have any chance of achieving anything then he had better get a move on. Since he was already thirteen and had, as yet, not really said anything.

Time and numbers.

Katarina wrote to me about them. She wrote about the experiments. Which were not something she was carrying out. But which were being carried out upon her.

2

TWO WEEKS AFTER we had become separated it was announced that the school would be offering a certain number of children in each class the opportunity of being examined by the school psychologist. By this they meant normal pupils. And, in addition, a number of those for whom special circumstances came into play and who were already going for examinations or check-ups.

The announcement was made in a letter that was sent to pupils' homes.

With pupils under fifteen – if they had no home, or if there was no way of contacting the family – no warning was given. They were simply advised that they had been selected for examination.

With those pupils over fifteen years of age, the letter was addressed to them personally. That must have been how Katarina knew about it. She must have received a letter about it.

The contents of letters from the school were not something you talked about. It was a rule. Even so it was impossible, in the long run, to avoid word getting out. Absence from class was very rare and only on production of a note from home. But now you could tell that something was up. You noticed straight away when totally normal pupils were suddenly absent during certain periods.

Rumour had it they were up seeing Hessen.

But even before the rumour had spread, I knew. Katarina had written to me about it.

"Binet-Simon?"

That was her first letter. That was all it said. She handed it to me between the ground floor and the first floor after the bell had rung, when we were making our way up the stairs. It was the only possible place.

That is true. It was the only place. Those thirty seconds from when we left the playground and ascended towards the first floor, where we would separate and she would climb higher; that was our only chance, in space and in time.

There was also the lunch break. But there the risk was too great.

It lasted from 11.40 to 12.30. For the first twenty minutes you sat in the classroom and ate your packed lunch. Lunch was only supervised by a teacher up to and including Primary VI. From Primary VII onwards there was no supervision. So it would have been possible to see one another then.

But we never chanced it, we would have been seen, people would have seen us. Sooner or later we would have been reported.

Tale-telling was frowned upon at Biehl's. But all pupils were encouraged to report any serious irregularities to the office or to their class teacher. Under the heading of serious irregularities came stealing – for example, if a pupil actually stole from other pupils' satchels – vandalism in the toilets – the only places not under constant supervision – smoking and breaking school rules, as for example when people had been forbidden to talk to one another.

At the Royal Orphanage you were also encouraged to report things. But there it almost never happened. Those few times when it did, you waited for a bit until the teachers relaxed their vigilance, and then made the informer jump from the willow tree into the lake, and did not haul out whoever it was until the moment where he had only just survived.

This rule did not exist at Biehl's. But then most of the pupils came from caring families and ran no special risk of being reported for anything. They had never needed to protect themselves, the way you do when you are on the borderline.

You never saw anyone being reported, it was done anonymously. Even so, you sensed that it happened pretty often. August and

Katarina must have sensed it too. We did not talk to one another in the corridor.

On the stairs she had managed to drop behind the rest of her class. You could not say that she touched me. But I knew there would be a letter.

She always kept her back very straight, even going upstairs. I knew I was no shorter than her. One year and eleven months and four days younger – I had looked it up in the year book – but not shorter. Taller, more like. At least, if I straightened up. I had tried, but it did not feel good – like cramp – so I had abandoned the idea.

She was past me even before I was really aware of her. She was wearing a black duffel coat.

Before we became separated, when I saw her in the courtyard with Biehl and then later on, I had never given a thought to the clothes she wore – other than that they were brilliant. Since then, the past few weeks, after we had become separated, perhaps never to talk to one another again, I had noticed how, more often than not, she went around in old clothes. Like grown-ups', but second-hand. Big sweaters with leather patches on the elbows. Or the black duffel coat.

One day I noticed that there were some men's things among them. And then I knew that some of these clothes must have belonged to her father; her mother too, maybe.

I could not get the idea out of my head. Every time I saw her. The straight back and the outsize clothes. Which had been her father's, who had hanged himself. Strong, and yet a bit lost. It was an inexplicable contradiction.

Maybe it is wrong to imagine that contradictions can be explained.

"Binet-Simon?"

She had written these words at the top of a sheet of paper, beneath them there was space for an reply.

I wrote "Yes".

Then two days went by before I had a chance to pass the note to her. I came up behind her on the stairs and slipped it into her duffel coat pocket. No one noticed anything. At first I thought she had not noticed. Then she put her hand up to her hair and pulled it free of her sweater and let it fall down her back. Then she waved to me. With the same hand that had touched her hair she waved to me, without turning round.

Two days went by before she sent me a reply. The reply was yet another question. She had written it on the same sheet, under my "Yes". It said: "Why is it not available?"

Before this I had never tried exchanging notes with anyone. I had seen others do it, but had never, personally, been involved.

Sometimes people had passed notes to one another in class. Maybe because they could not wait, maybe because it was hard to find a place where you were not being watched, maybe because they were bored. I had purposely avoided looking at what was in them.

One of these had been confiscated, by Fredhøj. No punishment had been meted out. Instead he had read the note out loud. It had been about love. You felt so ashamed, even though it was not your note. You felt as if you could have beaten up the one who had written it.

So now I felt uneasy. But I answered her anyway.

"Why is it not available?"

She had done what several others had done. She had looked up Binet-Simon in the school's card index which was in the library, right out in the open. You were encouraged to use it. It provided a complete listing of the school's collection of books and other printed matter. In the card index, just as at Crusty House, it said: "Not available."

Binet-Simon was an intelligence test; the one most commonly used in Denmark, and maybe in Europe as a whole. It was French, but adapted for the Danish system. On the front cover it said: "Danish standardised revision of Binet-Simon's intelligence tests by Marie Kirkelund and Sofie Rifbjerg. Revised, 1943."

Underneath this it said: "These tests are confidential. Publication, even in the form of extracts, is forbidden."

Which was why in the card index they were designated "Not available".

I knew this because it so happened that they had given them to me several times.

The second time was when they came out from Århus social services department to check whether it could be recommended that I sit the entrance exam for Crusty House.

The only way you could get into Crusty House was by having a mother who was a single parent, which I did not, or by being academically gifted – which, before now, no one at Himmelbjerg House had ever been. So, when it was mentioned to the social services department, they came out personally to check. And they brought Binet-Simon.

I had been given it some years earlier, in connection with the first escape attempts. They tested me then. This had not been entered in my file.

So I was already familiar with the test. And when I was waiting in the office and they went out to fetch a stopwatch I opened their briefcase. This was before the days of combination locks, it was a standard lock. I was hoping I could manage to get some of the answers off by heart, it had become very necessary to get out of there.

Just after that they came back. I did not get to see the answers, but I did manage to see the cover.

Since then I had been tested with Binet-Simon at Crusty House and by Hessen. Maybe they did not know I was familiar with it, maybe they thought that it made no difference. There was a test for each age level, which meant that each year you were given new, and unfamiliar, questions.

I tried to put some of this in my letter to Katarina.

*   *   *

Writing to her took a long time. One was not used to it, and it was hard to do it without being spotted. I did it at night. I tried to write precisely and accurately, but still it was upsetting to see one's own handwriting under hers. After a while I stopped trying and just answered her.

She kept asking about the tests.

At Crusty House they had started giving pupils their test results shortly after I was admitted, in 1968. Until then they had been kept secret. You solved the problems and you knew you were being evaluated, but you were never told anything.

I had been there six months when we started getting the results. It was at this time, too, that I was given partial insight into my file. They explained that it had to do with a new teaching method.

The result you were given consisted of a figure and a classification. Different from test to test. Binet-Simon told you how many per cent below the national average your intelligence lay. Jepsen's speech and language test told you how fluent you were – they used a tape recorder and afterwards they wrote down what you had said and counted your pauses, and measured the length of the words you used. In this way they could measure how complex your language was – the fewer the pauses, the longer the words, the greater your fluency. In the Danish Institute of Education's standardised reading proficiency tests they measured the number of mistakes and the reading speed. This gave two figures which could then be compared with the national average for that particular age level.

At Crusty House you never talked about the tests, only ever about the results.

Katarina did not write about her results, not once. She wrote about the actual problems.

She wrote: "Are they all timed?"

To this I could reply in the affirmative. Binet-Simon had six tests for each age level. The last three were timed. You had ten or fifteen minutes to read a story – about a grasshopper, for example. You had to insert the missing syllables. But even with the first three, lesser, problems, they kept an eye on the clock.

At Himmelbjerg House and Crusty House they had had a special psychologists' clock in the room where they did the tests. Big, a bit like the ones they use in ball games. They set it going when the test began, it was turned away from you, only the psychologist had been able to see it. Hessen used a combined wristwatch and stopwatch. It took a little time for me to realise this. She could start and stop it and read off the time in such a way that you almost missed it.

In Jepsen's speech and language test you had two minutes in which to talk about a picture. In the standardised reading tests classification was by your year.

This is what I wrote back to her. I also asked her to destroy this sheet of paper. We were still using the same one; with all that was now written on it, if it were confiscated, it would mean the end.

Binet-Simon was used to calculate the intelligence quotient. They started with tests just below your age level and worked downwards until you could solve all the problems. Then they worked upwards until you could not solve any of the problems. In this way they could calculate your mental age. At Hessen's mine had been 12.9 – one year and one month younger than I actually was. This figure was then divided by my actual age and multiplied by 100. So, mental age divided by actual age multiplied by 100 equalled intelligence. Mine was just over 92, in other words, average intelligence. From 90 to 110 you were of average intelligence.

The limit for being transferred from Himmelbjerg House was set at 75. If you had an intelligence quotient of less than 75 but more than 72 you were sent to a residential school for the mildly retarded. If you had less than 72 you came under mental retardation services and were sent to the loony bin.

So the test results were always related to time. Thereby producing a new figure – a measurement of intelligence. A calculated figure, and hence quite objective. All the psychologist had done was to let the children read and answer the questions, record them on a tape, note the times, double-check the figures and refer to the evaluation table. Everything clear and obvious. So that the result was, by and large, exempt from human uncertainty.

Almost scientific.

A week went by, and no letter.

In the afternoons, during free time, I would walk down through the grounds to the gate and watch the cars go by. There were children in some of them, on their way home with their parents. From the gate you could see the girls' wing in the annexe.

Other than that I just stayed in my room, over in the corner, with the light out. One felt a bit like an animal in its lair, like a fox.

I thought about August and the kitchen, even though he had been taken from me and so was no longer my responsibility. One night I went across to the sickbay. The door was locked. Not a sound to be heard. During classes there was no chance of talking to him, they kept a close eye on us.

A letter came from her. It was not in her own words, it was a quote straight out of Binet-Simon. She must have learnt it by heart, just by reading it. "There was once a grasshopper, who had sung merrily all summer long. Now it was winter and he was starving. So he went to see some ants who lived nearby and asked them to lend him some of the stores they had laid up for the winter. 'What have you been doing all summer?' they asked. 'I have sung day and night,' replied the grasshopper. 'Ah, so you have sung,' said the ants. 'Well, now you can dance.' "

Beneath this she had written: "What is the moral?"

It was so deep. It showed how she had figured out that this was a problem from the "fourteen years" level and that I must have had it. She had, therefore, used what I had written to her and discovered the system behind Binet-Simon.

At the time when I had been given this story, I had come close to answering that the moral was, ants were not helpful. But this would not have fitted in very well with the other problems. Instead I had sussed out Hessen and then I had said the moral was that one must make hay while the sun shines.

I had been able to see from her face that this was the correct answer.

Reading between the lines of Katarina's letter I understood that she, too, had been about to give the wrong answer. That was why she sent it to me. She knew that we had both been about to give the wrong answer.

I knew that our letters were part of her experiment with time. That she was trying to understand. That, in a way, we were in the laboratory when we wrote. Even though we were prevented from talking to one another.

It was easier to get up in the morning when you had received a letter and had to reply. Writing to her, I understood things I had not previously understood. You were surprised by your own replies.

In a way that is what I have been trying to do ever since.

Later on, Binet-Simon did become available to me. I borrowed it from the Danish Teacher Training College at 101 Emdrupvej, where they have it in their collection of tests. It is still in use.

It says in the foreword that "if every case of mild retardation were recognised in time, and the child or young person treated in accordance with the result produced by the psychological examination, the number of mental defectives committing offences would rapidly be reduced."

Still, even today, there is a ban on quoting from it. Nevertheless I am doing so. No harm intended.

They wanted to help. It is down there in black and white, in the foreword to Binet-Simon, but this was something you already knew, back then. They wanted to help children and society. By pinpointing those who were mildly retarded, or downright defective, in order that they could be sent to residential schools or homes where they could be given the necessary care. That was the idea. They wanted to help the victims of evolution. They waited, just like Biehl, under the archway. So that they could single out those who were on the borderline, who could not finish the tests in time, and help them up. They wanted to take people under their wings.

They were also the ravens.

This is a contradiction. I have no explanation.

They believed that it was of great help to children to be assessed.

I suppose they still believe that. In our society it is a pretty widespread belief. That assessment is a good thing.

I was at the playground with the child. These days I am more often alone with her, usually we go out.

When you are moving, or at a playground, then you feel that you are achieving something for her. When you are at home, just sitting with her and not knowing what to do, then comes the fear; then you have a clear sense of your own inadequacy.

We were at the playground, she had climbed up on to some railway sleepers. She was about one metre off the ground. She called to me from there.

"Look!"

I did not get the answer out. I had no time. It came from a stranger – she was also there with her child.

"What a clever girl!" she said.

I had no time to think. I was on my feet and on my way over to bite her head off. Then I remembered that she was the mother of a small child and that she was a woman. I realised that I was having a relapse.

I sat down, but it was a long time before I stopped shaking.

The child had wanted attention. She had just asked to be noticed. But she was given an assessment. "What a clever girl!"

When you assess others, no harm is ever intended. It is just that you yourself have been tested so often. In the end it is impossible to think any other way.

Maybe it is not so easy to see if you have always been able to achieve more or less what has been required of you. Maybe you see it best if you know that, all through your life, you will always be on the borderline.

Katarina's last letter had to do with Raven's progressive matrices. Those I could not help her with, they were for highly intelligent children and beyond. I had heard rumours about them, but never seen them.

I managed to receive this letter, but not to reply to it. It happened in church. Where we were found out, and where the letter was confiscated. After that, separation was absolute.

3

THERE WERE FOUR compulsory church services a year – Advent, Christmas, Easter and Whitsun. You were escorted to the church by the teacher you had had just before. We had had Flage Biehl for arithmetic.

Usually you were allowed just to get on with it by yourself, doing sums from your book. They were quiet classes.

Nevertheless, it was important that your work was neat, and that you held the paper steady when you were rubbing out, to stop it getting creased. That was his weak spot.

He had the reputation of being a sensitive soul. Often, when he had hit someone because of a messy jotter, he was unable to proceed – despite the fact that he had been in the middle of a lesson. Instead he would remain at his desk, sitting there with his head bowed for the rest of the period.

Before we became separated I had tried to explain to August the importance of being neat. Then he had become very hard.

"A pigsty," he said, "that's what she says. When I'm at home I sleep in the living room, on a camp bed. I draw when they're asleep. Sometimes the crayons are crumbly. If she finds even the tiniest speck she starts to cry and says it's a pigsty. All for a tiny fleck of crayon. Apart from that no one has ever seen her cry."

I had not referred to it again. I did not want to pry. But I think he tried to do better. Just as he had filled in the background.

Even so, it had not been good enough. When Flage came into the class his face was bright red. He was carrying a bundle of jotters which he had corrected. He dropped them on to the desk and picked up the top one. Then he came over to our desk.

He must have been warned about keeping a safe distance from August, but he was so angry that he had forgotten himself.

"Trash," he said, he was having trouble talking.

He hit August with the jotter, from right to left, knocking August's head sideways. Then he hit it from the other side, knocking it back again. He kept this up for some time. He never touched people, he always hit them with their own jotter, wherein lay the untidiness.

His blows were not in the same class as Biehl's or Karin Ærø's. Nevertheless they were effective, because the jotter, as it were, lengthened his reach. And, at the same time, the humiliation was greater because he would not touch people.

Afterwards, he threw the jotter on the floor.

This was the first time August had been hit at the school. The instant the jotter hit the floor he was on his feet, very fast.

Some people never learned how to take a beating. It was not so much a case of whether you had been brought up in an institution or with a family, but more whether you had been getting clouted from when you were pretty small, and had learned that the best strategy was just to bear in mind that you take it and then it is over and done with.

August would never learn, that I already knew. When Flage hit him that first time, he seized up; the head moved from side to side, but the body was rigid. I came up behind him, I sensed what was going to happen.

He went for Flage's fingers, which had remained in midair after he had thrown the jotter. He grabbed hold of the outer two on his left hand, but did not get the chance to break them. I stuck a thumb over each of his eyes and pulled him back. He did not utter a sound, he was hard as wood. Then I sat him down on his chair. Flage was looking at his fingers, he had no idea what had happened.

This brought the lesson to a halt. Flage left the classroom. It had happened before. It was unlikely that he would go up to the office and report August. He was new in class; Flage must have known he had gone too far. But he was compelled to leave, due to his sensitivity.

I took August out into the corridor. It was deserted, all the other classes were in the middle of a lesson. I let him pace along the walls.

"You've stopped eating," I said.

I had noticed this a while before but had said nothing.

"It's a trial period," he said, "here at the school. I'm here on trial, I'm not going to make it."

Of this there had been no previous mention.

How long was the trial period, I asked him.

"They haven't said," he said. "Some decisions have been taken about me, they've told me that much, but they haven't said what."

We had not spoken to one another in a fortnight. I felt that we had better make the most of it, and the corridor was deserted. What had they said they were after, I asked him, what was he supposed to do?

"Make a go of it," he said. "They said it was a trial period, it would give me a chance to prove that I can make a go of it."

"Where will they send you if it goes wrong?" I said.

"Back to Sandbjerggård."

There was no chance to ask about anything else. The new superintendent came to get us and walked us down to the church. Flage must have sent for her.

A fortnight earlier, they had taken over an empty room in the girls' section, and workmen had been called in. She had arrived a few days later, and was bidden welcome at Assembly. It was said that, among other things, she would be put in temporary charge of the girls' section in the annexe, just as Flakkedam was in charge of the boys'. It was the first time mention had been made of Flakkedam's supervisory post being temporary.

No more had been said.

The church was just outside the grounds.

We were on our way up the aisle. Katarina came up to us. Suddenly she was at August's side. She reached behind him and put something in my pocket. It was the letter. I would not have read it there and then, but it was some days since I had heard from her, and, with so many people around, you felt hidden. I unfolded it right away. It was quite short, she was asking about Raven's progressive matrices.

I looked up at her.

"August is here on trial," I said. "He doesn't know for how long, he doesn't know what they have decided about him, he's not going to make it. It's getting worse day by day, what can be done?"

"His file," she said.

We were squashed up against one another, by everybody else, and so that no one could see us.

"Any decisions they've taken have to be entered in it," she said.

Just as she said it, there was Fredhøj.

I was the one who should have been on the lookout. I was the only one who really knew him. But I had forgotten myself, and he had always been very quick – invisible and yet, all of a sudden, on the spot.

He took the letter from me. Then he took me and Katarina and put us in separate pews. Then he fetched August. He did not come at him from the front, but went round behind him, pinioned his wrists and brought him down to the row in front of me, and sat him down next to himself. No one had sensed anything. It had all been as smooth and casual as if he were showing people to their seats.

He could have marched us out right there and then, but he did not. Instead we were put in the pews and the service went ahead as though nothing had happened.

While one sat there knowing that it was all over.

Fredhøj had known that now he would have us hit by Ragnarok – he would have us obliterated. Still he had strength enough to sit down as though nothing had happened and let the service begin. Strength enough to make this eloquent pause.

So now one could sit there, looking round at everybody else. One could think about how, if one had respected the school rules and not abused the trust placed in one, one could have been singing away like them right now. Then one could still have been on the borderline instead of, as now, being lost.

Thoughts like that might run through your mind. That was the intention behind the pause.

There was another reason, too. They could afford to wait,

because the harm had already been done, and we had been located. The fact is, somewhere there was this anger, this hostility towards us, so huge that it could afford to wait. Anger that was not Fredhøj's, nor even Biehl's. They were, when all was said and done, human and capable of letting bygones be bygones – one had seen several instances of it. This anger was different. It was the anger of the very school itself, greater than anything human. It did not forget, it would remember for ever.

I came close to giving up.

It was impossible to think straight. Surrender gripped one like an illness one could not, personally, do anything about.

I thought about what would happen to me and Katarina. But mostly I thought about August. I could see now that he had been given a trial period, not just at Biehl's but with the world. He had been given a trial period just to go on living. He was like a very small and very sick wild animal that was only just managing to keep going. If he were sent back to a place like Sandbjerggård it would be the end of him. They would shut him up so tightly that he would be crushed to death.

A hymn was sung: "Sometimes a light surprises". Biehl himself led the singing, before the minister took over.

You had always been able to sense that this hymn held some special meaning for him. When he sang it he came very close to something crucial. He had expounded upon it.

> ". . . Who gives the lilies clothing
> Will clothe his people too:
> Beneath the spreading heavens
> No creature but is fed;
> And he who feeds the ravens
> Will give his children bread."

Referring to this verse, he had said that when biology and science were powerless, then God prevailed.

*   *   *

It was like being in a little cage, with the walls closing in and all the doors shut. Humlum and Axel Fredhøj had given up long ago, along with many another one had known. And there had been many times when one had almost done so. And yet I had held out, longer than most, I had done my best. At the Orphanage, the first time I was made to jump from the willow tree, just after I came there – when they waited a long time before bringing me up – I had come close to going along with it and letting the water fill my lungs. But back then I believed that in the end one would come up into the light. One no longer had that feeling of certainty.

I looked around for one last time, to consign my thoughts to the air. That is when I saw August, he was sitting next to Fredhøj, all hunched up.

It was still too early to let go. One still had to help him. When one is bigger than someone else, and not so sensitive, and can take being hit, and has discerned the grand plan, then one has to help someone who is smaller than oneself.

I looked around the cage. All the doors were locked. In my affliction my thoughts turned to Jesus.

You had always imagined God as being like Biehl. As a rule He was distant. As a rule He concerned himself with the greatest and the smallest. Like the heavens, or a lily. Only rarely did He ever address himself to you in person. And then, as a rule, it was in order to punish.

Until now I had thought of Jesus as being like Fredhøj. Standing between you and the supreme power, Biehl and God, there had to be some kind of a middleman, an informer. Fredhøj and Jesus.

It had been the same everywhere. At the top the headmaster or the superintendent, between him and the rest of the school a deputy. It was a law, maybe even a law of nature.

Then another thought occurred.

You had always learned the prayers and hymns by heart. It had been like memorising dates, like the Battle of Poitiers, only easier, because they rhymed and there was a tune.

As a rule you did not make much sense of the words. However,

Biehl had been known, out of the blue, to conduct a test on one of the hymns. If he then detected a lack of understanding he became very dangerous. As a rule he would then explain certain things, like the bit about clothing the lily. But there were too many prayers and hymns for them all to be explained. So you learned them off by heart, without making much sense of them.

Even so it could happen that you suddenly understood, all by yourself. That the words you had learned by heart became a door, opening up.

That happened now.

God was too close to Biehl. Nor could you consult Jesus about your personal problems, there was no reason to believe that you would be given help. In fact there were really no instances of anyone being given help.

And yet, my thoughts turned to Jesus. Well, you had learned it by heart and been made to recite it, albeit without making much sense of it. There were two things I remembered. Jesus had talked about time. People had asked him whether he could promise them eternal life, in other words freedom from time. He had not really answered that. Like Katarina, when I had asked her in the laboratory whether I could be sure of being cured and she had not given a straight answer. Instead he had told the young man who had asked the question what he should do if he wanted to enter into life, here and now.

Jesus had been asked about eternity. And he had pointed to the here and now. It had never been explained, the Bible was full of things like that. Biehl read from it at Assembly, but it was never explained.

What should you do if you would enter into life, here and now? This was what Jesus had answered. That was one of the things I thought about.

The other was that maybe Jesus had also tried to touch time, maybe that had been his plan. In his laboratory, not in the manger but later on, he had gathered his thoughts to understand the plan behind it all. Then he had told those who followed him that they must go forth into the world and reveal this plan, even though the natural aversion of the people would be roused against them, so that they would be persecuted and isolated. This they should do so that everything that was covert should be revealed. Then he had descended into the underworld.

Descent into the underworld. And so I made up my mind.

Fredhøj sat diagonally in front of me, his hands resting on the ledge for the hymn book in front of him. One hand lay across the other, you could smell his shaving lotion. All in all, the sense of him was overwhelming.

Across his left hand lay his key ring. As always.

All the locks in the school were linked to a comprehensive master-key system. A Ruko system – back then there was nothing else.

The keys were in order of precedence. At the top, a master key – held by Biehl alone – which opened every door in the school. Then came the sub-master keys held by Fredhøj and Flakkedam and the new superintendent; beneath them came the departmental keys and, at the bottom, the keys held by the ordinary teachers.

It was a good system, with only one flaw. At its lower levels, as for example with the main door and the doors to the corridors, it was necessary that a number of different keys could open each lock. The more keys that have to fit a lock, the weaker it is, the more receptive to alien keys.

I could not have done it today. Apart from the fact that today I would never have wanted to, still, it could not have been done. Advances in technology have made it impossible.

In those days, they were ordinary five-pin keys, the cuts of the key fitted into the lock and pushed five bottom pins into place, then the cylinder could move freely. Nowadays, with the modern systems that time and technology have produced, there are also side pins. In addition to which the keys are patented and the designs restricted. I could not have done it today.

I looked at Fredhøj's keys.

Of course I had known they were there. But I had deliberately avoided taking a closer look at them.

On the bunch were some standard keys, as well as several smaller keys to the locks of the physics cupboards. Then there were the Yale keys to his home. And his car keys. The school key was lying awkwardly, but I just waited. There came a moment when he shifted position and it was brought into full view.

I concentrated on the depth of the cuts – nothing else. Afterwards I closed my eyes. And sort of tested myself on the key. As thoughIhadbeenupattheblackboard.

At last I had it.

None of us were expelled. There was absolutely no accounting for it.

That very evening they moved August out of the dining room and served him his food in his room, in the sickbay. The next day they moved him down a class and put Flakkedam on permanent watch over him. To begin with Katarina was absent – I thought for ever – but a few days later I saw her in the playground, sitting on a bench, looking down at the tarmac. As for me, I was summoned to the secretary's office. Fredhøj and Karin Ærø were there, and Stuus – in his capacity as chairman of the board of teachers. They advised me that I had been reported to the Children's Panel and to the child welfare services, since I was on a scholarship and had been given special permission to attend the school. There would now be a pause. When the reply from my guardian and from the Department of Health and Welfare was available, they would review the situation.

Karin Ærø did the talking. She was our class teacher. Fredhøj stayed absolutely still. I tried to suss him out, the situation was absolutely inexplicable. Even though I had been given my final warning, they had still not kicked me out. There was no understanding it.

$$4$$

THE FIRST TIME Biehl talked about the Battle of Poitiers he had made an additional remark. That had been only the second time ever that he referred to himself as "I".

There had been a pause, after which he had said that it was his personal opinion that Islam, which was the religion of the Moors, was nothing less than the devil's own work. So, the Battle of Poitiers had been a struggle between the forces of light and of darkness. And if the struggle had turned out to the Moors' advantage, civilisation as we know it would never have existed.

This was the only thing about the devil that had ever been explained outright at the school.

Even so, there was no doubt in your mind. When we descended those seven steps into the darkness, and pushed aside the panel, you knew you were going down into the underworld.

I did not collect August until I could almost sense the breathing of both Flakkedam and the new superintendent. The clock said seven minutes past midnight.

It was ten days since we had spoken to one another and had been found out in church. I had not seen August, other than at Assembly and from a distance in the playground.

I made hardly any sound opening the door. He had grown very thin. Under different circumstances he should have been reported so that he could have been made to eat.

I told him he had to get up, but gave him no further explanation. He was in his pyjamas and slippers, they kept his clothes and outdoor shoes locked up at night.

*　　　*　　　*

We had woodwork once a week. The woodwork room was on the first floor and the metalwork tools were also kept there. Klastersen was the woodwork teacher. The year before, Carsten Sutton had been caught sniffing solvents – cellulose thinner. It was kept in a thirty-litre container, you could get your whole head into it. We had all tried it, but he was the one who got found out, due to the fact that he had gone berserk afterwards. Since then Klastersen kept a pretty close eye on people.

I had shown him a cracked table-tennis bat. "May I have permission to repair this?" I said. There had been no problem, not when it was sports equipment.

I had found a place for myself beside a vice at the very back. Then I had cut out Fredhøj's key in sheet metal as best I could from memory. Over the next few days I had tried it out and made some adjustments to it.

Now I let August and myself out through the main door. It was a frosty night, but there was no snow. We left no tracks.

The art room was seven steps down on a stairway that started just beyond the main door under the archway. On the way down there were two doors, one to stop pupils from hanging about on the stairs – out of sight of the teacher on playground duty – and then the actual door to the art room. Both came under the master-key system.

For a long time I had believed that I was the only one who knew about the way down to the service corridors. But Axel Fredhøj must have known about it, too. That was how he had made his descent, although he must have locked the door behind him, they brought him up on the playground side, they had no idea how he had got down there. He cannot have told them either, otherwise the opening would have been blocked up. Maybe he was tougher than people thought; maybe he was just not in a condition to say anything special, not even when he was questioned.

*   *   *

It was no secret that the corridors existed.

When the new toilets were built, the school's parents had been encouraged to help with the demolition of the old ones – to save money, and to emphasise the especially caring nature of those parents connected to the school.

I took part on that occasion – to see peoples' parents. Usually you never saw them close up.

Besides which you had been given the chance of tearing down. You had been handed a sledgehammer, then you could just bash away.

An architect's drawing of the school had been hung on the wall, so that you could see how it would look with the new toilets. Which would have tiles and lights and be in decent working order, not all black and filthy and stinking like the old ones.

The service corridors were shown on the drawings. I had noticed them because it was only a month since the accident. The first of Axel Fredhøj's two accidents, that is.

The corridors ran six metres underground, two metres below the basement. Through them ran the heating pipes, hot water pipes and electricity cables. But not gas. That was what you could see.

The opening must have come about because they built the art room late on, a long time after the school, maybe as part of the new trend in education. So all they had done was to build a partition out of hardboard – by the look of it, it had been a rush job. This tied in with the order of precedence governing subjects. Art came right at the bottom, even lower than weaving and domestic science. No year was ever given marks for art.

And yet Karin Ærø was the art teacher. Although she, for example, never handled clay. She also taught music and Danish, and music and literature were clearly closest to her heart.

I lit a little candle and placed it in an aluminium cylinder with little windows of clear plastic and air holes at the bottom, it was one I had kept from the old days. August was close beside me, maybe he could not see very well. When I struck the match he went rigid, but then relaxed again.

Behind the panel lay a bricked-in space with no windows. Even the floor was brick. It was cold. In the floor was a black hole – the descent to the corridors.

They must have forgotten about this way down when they were doing the building. Doors blocked the outlets to the north and south playgrounds, there were iron bars strung with wire netting over the air vents. Even so, they had not succeeded in making it absolutely secure.

To get down you had to step on to the lagging around the pipes and from there slide down into the tunnel itself. There was little or no headroom. Even I, with my natural stoop, kept bumping my head on the roof.

It was warmer here, because of the pipes. There was a humming sound, from the boiler maybe.

On our left the lagging around the pipes was still black.

August took my hand.

"I'm afraid of the dark," he said.

I stayed where I was. I could not go on until I had told him about it. Even though he was smaller than me, like a child, I had to tell him.

I told him straight. One day a boy from the school – that was Axel – had hidden in the art room and got himself locked in on purpose. He had taken a bottle of benzine from there and, in the lunch break, he had descended into the tunnel. There he had poured the benzine over the lagging around the pipes, then he had set a match to it, and then he had lain down beside the fire.

"You can't lie still when there's a fire burning," said August.

But that what was what he had done. No details had ever been released, but there were those who had heard what the firemen said when they brought him up – by the stairs to the playground. It was from there, too, that the smoke had been spotted.

"So," said August, "what happened to him?"

I replied that nothing had happened. They had spotted the smoke and rung the fire brigade. They had brought him up. Other than that, nothing had happened. Other than that he had stopped driving home from school with his father.

No one had ever seen Axel and Fredhøj speak to one another. If you had not known it, you would never have guessed that they were father and son. They had, however, gone home from school together. After school, on Wednesdays and Fridays, when their timetables must have coincided, they drove home together in Fredhøj's big Rover – out through the grounds and away. Axel sat in the back.

After the accident, this stopped. Instead Axel was collected by his mother, Fredhøj's wife.

She picked him up at the gate to the road. She had a Rover like Fredhøj's, she too was a deputy superintendent, elsewhere in the suburbs. She drove up to the gate and Axel got into the back. They drove away without a word having been said.

It was the first time you had seen her. But Fredhøj had mentioned her before.

It cropped up in a period where he had been reading aloud. He was not in the habit of reading aloud – the maths and physics syllabus was too full to allow for that. But he had been known, around Christmas time, to step up the pace. You took on more arithmetic homework, thus gaining a couple of hours in which he would read aloud.

He was brilliant at it. He always read stories about great and intelligent criminals; stories from *Crime Cavalcade* or *From Foreign Courts* and *Great and Notorious Swindlers*. It was after having read a story about a bigamist that he mentioned his wife, Axel's mother.

This man had murdered women by raising their ankles while they were in the bath. They had been able to keep their heads above water for a while, but eventually they had given up, so they drowned. Then he had inherited their fortunes and married again.

After closing the book Fredhøj had stared into space for a moment. You could sense that he was close to something crucial. Lack of intelligence, he had said, was to blame for the fact that most people had such trouble with marriage. For their part, he and his wife had organised things in such a way that they split their time. She had made the decisions for the first ten years: where they should live, what kind of cars they should have – hence the Rovers. Then there had been ten years during which he had made the decisions. These had now come to an end and it was once more her turn to decide.

Teachers seldom or never spoke about what went on in their families. This was the first time Fredhøj had said any such thing.

That they had split their time. Almost scientifically.

I had tried to work it out. I came to the conclusion that Fredhøj's wife must have decided on Axel.

I tried to explain this to August. It was hard to tell whether he was listening. I did not dare to talk above a whisper, and all the while he kept pacing alongside the pipes. Never far away though, only as far as the rim of darkness.

I paused, and he stopped.

"That wasn't what I meant," he said. "Why did he do it? What was the matter with him?"

What was the matter with him? Nothing much, really, I said. He was fine, really, until the incident with the chart locker six months later, and could we get a move on, there was something we had to do.

He stayed where he was. He stood there, touching the lagging.

"Clothes can't hardly burn," he said.

No, I said, that was what had saved Axel, and could we go now. I tried moving on with the light, to get him to follow. Then he turned towards me. He did not look straight at me, but I could see there was something he had to say, it was hard to get it out. At the Orphanage you often had haemorrhoids – it was the food that did it. That was how it felt, like bleeding piles, but it has to come out. It hurt, but there was no alternative.

"I don't put up with anything," he said, "not from anyone. They come home, and you're lying in the camp bed. You could have run off, but then he would have felt cheated. They start to say things. Usually it's about the report card and the drawings. A pigsty, she says. Do something about your son. She eggs him on, know what I mean?"

I said nothing.

"He tosses lighted matches on to the duvet. You just have to lie still, as if you're sleeping. It doesn't catch fire, fabric doesn't burn well. Then they come. You could run from them, but he would feel cheated. It has to be as if . . ."

"An achievement and a reward," I said.

"That's it. You have to let him catch you, or else there'll be hell to pay. He holds you down, but she's the one who does it. Always with a coat hanger, down the back. And then, at the very end, on the bare arse, y'know. I just happened to think of it. Forget it."

We stood there, saying nothing. He was not finished yet.

"I don't put up with anything," he said. "I've warned them. They've done it for the last time."

He had started shaking.

"I could adopt you," I said, "when I'm twenty-one. You could come and live with us, with me and Katarina."

The shaking came from the inside, but it was much bigger than the tiny, skinny body. I set the lamp down on the pipe and reached for his hand.

It happened too fast to do anything about it. I heard the sound before I felt anything. It was the little finger he broke, it made the same sound as when you snap a pencil. When the pain came, it brought me to my knees. He had not let go, he kept on squeezing. Now he was looking straight down at me, I do not think he knew who I was. The other August had taken over, there was hardly anything left of the first one.

"No one's going to touch me," he said.

He pressed down on my finger and looked me in the eye, to see the pain.

"D'you know what it's like in the end?" he said. "In the end it's great. If she keeps going long enough, it gets so it's lovely, and you want to ask her to keep going. But by then you can hardly talk. And then you faint."

I could sense that I was going to pass out, so I pressed my forehead against the floor. When I looked up he had let go of me and drawn back into himself. He was standing over by the lamp, with his back to me, looking into the flame.

*　　　*　　　*

My plan had been for us to climb out through a vent at the foot of the south stairway. We found it alright, but it turned out to be covered over with wire netting. Normally I could have pulled away the netting, but, because of my finger, this was now out of the question.

So we wandered about a bit. There were more tunnels than I had remembered from the drawing, most were dead ends, but some went round in a circle. At one point I had to change the candle.

There was no question of giving up, I was responsible for August. At one point, when I changed the candle I almost lost him in the dark, then he took my good hand. And I let him, though I tried to watch out for my fingers.

Eventually we came up through the landing pit.

Klastersen taught PE and woodwork. He had been appointed the year before. He had been trainer of the cubs for the national handball team, and was highly qualified. He had said that his training programme would concentrate on building up the front. In six months' time we would all have a strong front. Work on the gym apparatus was particularly well-suited to this, he said, and most especially the mastering of high flights and deep landings. So he had put a ban on the use of the thick mats. By going barefoot and using the hard mats or coming down straight on to the floor you could build up a very hard front. But it was not long before several accidents occurred. When a boy called Kåre Frymand ripped both of his Achilles tendons in one go the school had been directed to use thick mats and install a landing pit.

The pit consisted of a box four metres by four, and three metres deep, set into the floor. It had been installed right after the accident and was supposed to have been filled with sawdust. This, however, had never been done and so day in and day out it just sat there, covered up.

And now we came up through it. It had been built down into the service corridors. In the bottom, on one side, there was a hatch. We came out of the gym on to the south stairway, which we then ascended.

It was very quiet. We had sort of sneaked up on the school, so it was not doing its job properly, it seemed to be paralysed.

And yet it had its eye on us, you sensed it. For the first time it struck me that the very building belonged to Biehl. The walls were watching us.

With the walls it was like this: they were not to be touched. There was a ban on leaning against walls and doorposts because of the wear and tear, Biehl himself had announced this at Assembly. He had always protected them, now they were staring at us.

But we ascended the stairs. I did it for August. I sensed that the law of reciprocation could not be a law of nature after all. When people were weak and helpless, like August for example, then it might be necessary to do something for them without getting anything in return. To do anything, no matter what.

And yet you did get something in return. I had descended and then ascended to help and protect him. Now it was as though he were helping me. As though you could set yourself free by helping others.

I cannot put it any better.

We got in through Hessen's clinic, it took some time to open the door into the next room.

I had never been in there before. It was pretty much as I had known it would be. Small, with shelves where she kept the balls and jigsaw puzzles used when examining the smaller pupils. And a grey filing cabinet.

I left it alone. We would not find what we were looking for here. Still I stood there for a moment, running a hand over it. You had known it was there, but never seen it.

August was standing behind me, absolutely still. I turned round to whisper something, or to motion to him that we had better get on.

And looked straight into the previous room, Hessen's clinic, which we had just left.

We had closed the door, August had done that. And yet we were both now looking through the wall and into the clinic. As though the wall had not been there.

It was August who stretched a hand out towards it. It was brought up short by something.

"It's glass," he said.

It was like a big window, but there was no reflection from the candle. The glass could not be seen, only felt.

"It's the back of the mirror," I said, "it's see-through."

There had been a few times when I had turned up at the clinic at the appointed time and it was not Hessen, but one of her assistants, who had been there. On those occasions the proceedings had been a little different. You had talked off the record about how things had been since last time.

Now I realised that, on these occasions, while you had just been relaxing and talking to the assistants, who were much younger than Hessen, she had been in this room, behind the mirror. She could sit in peace, observing the whole thing. It was brilliant.

Off the corridor on the fifth floor there were Biehl's office and the staff room and the library and the assembly hall and the district medical officer's clinic. A door led directly from the corridor into Biehl's office. Those who had been sent up for punishment had to wait outside this door. This saved them from causing any inconvenience in the school office, where the secretary sat. Then, too, it made the punishment worse if they had to stand in the corridor, where they could be seen by passing teachers.

The door came under the master-key system, but only Biehl's key fitted it, so the lock took a bit of time, especially since I could only use one hand. There was just a little bit of candle left. I blew it out, we would need the last of it for finding the papers.

When it went dark he huddled up against me.

"There's nothing for us here," he said.

His voice was unrecognisable.

I could not think of an answer for him.

"I'm going home," he said.

He started to walk out into the darkness and then to run. He must have forgotten where he was, he was running blind, but very fast. He hit a doorpost, but got up and ran on. At the end of the corridor he ran into the washbasin, I heard him hit it with his teeth.

I walked over to him. He was lying on his back, I could tell by touch that his mouth was bleeding. I could not carry him because of my hand, so I dragged him back. I took off my shirt and propped him up against the wall and got him to hold the shirt up to his mouth. Then I switched on the light.

It was risky, but there was nothing else for it.

Andersen – Lemmy, that is – lived in a little house on the other side of the south playground. In his hallway he had a panel of lamps that indicated where lights were burning in the school. It had been installed just after I came, most likely to save electricity. You could see it through his windows.

So I knew that now, when I pressed the switch, a light would come on in his house. But it had to be done.

The cleaning ladies at the school were specially selected and highly qualified. They had been appointed when Biehl started the school in humble premises on Jacoby's Allé in Frederiksberg, and had accompanied it on its rise. They were on familiar terms with the management of the school. They had always reported all traces of smoking, burnt celluloid or any other signs of vandalism. They saw things that other people did not see, it was very hard to hide anything from them, they would have spotted August's blood right away, I had to mop it up. I worked my way back along the corridor using my socks, it was all I had. Then I put them back on.

When I came back August was sitting looking at the door opposite, which led up to Biehl's flat. He had his private quarters on the top floor – this you knew, even though you had never been up there. The door to the stairs was opposite his office, with his name on it. It was the only door in the school with a name on it. To show that the ordinary part of the school stopped here. August sat there, looking at the nameplate and holding the shirt up to his mouth. He said not a word. I switched off the light and let us in to the office.

I had been there twice before. The first time had been when they introduced me to August. The other time, which had been earlier on, had been for punishment. That had been the first time I had been hit at Biehl's. I had been late five times in a month, it was at the time that my illness was getting worse.

It had been me and Jes Jessen and someone else. It was normal for Biehl to take two or three at once – to save time. There was a rug in the middle of the floor. "Stay off the rug," he had said. "Let's have no more wear and tear than we can avoid."

You had to stand with your hands behind your back, so you

would not try to protect your face. He walked back and forth while getting into his stride – on the rug, too. You had not heard the words, it was more as though I had noticed the colour of his skin, I had known when the blow was coming. Still it had taken you by surprise. Jes had fallen down, but I had stayed upright.

So now you automatically walked around the rug, and over to the desk. August went off into a corner. After he hurt himself he had calmed down, you could see he was very tired, which was due to the fact that he had not eaten.

It was a fairly simple matter to open the chest – it might never have been locked. Never, ever had they expected anyone to attempt such an offence. There were so many things they had thought of, they had safeguarded themselves against almost everything, but not against this.

Nor, under normal circumstances, should this have been done. By opening this chest you were abusing your fellow pupils' trust; you were acting in an underhand manner. The ravens on the lid reminded you of this. That there was a justice from which nothing could be hidden.

But at the moment the object was to protect August.

I did not switch on the light, the moon was bright. I could see the letters on the folders containing the documents. They were arranged alphabetically, like a telephone book but not packed so close together.

"The bell doesn't ring at night," said August.

Until he said it, it had never occurred to me.

"It's like she says," he said. "When it doesn't ring there's another time in this place. It's as if there is no time."

I pointed to the moon.

"Time's built into the world," I said. "The moon rises and sets, there's a system, like a clock."

"But it doesn't ring a bell every fifty minutes," he said.

The folder was thick, I lit the candle. He did not come any closer.

"Whose business is it anyway?" he said. "Huh?"

One folder held his school record. He had gone to a normal school on Slotsherrensvej in Rødovre. I flicked past these folders. Then came the test results from the examinations by the school psychologist, and the case sheet from the school doctor. Then came something from the social services department and two folders from the child psychiatric unit at University Hospital – they had examined him twice. I did not look at any of this. Last but one came the papers from Biehl's – a number of letters. First time round I let them pass. Last of all came some typewritten sheets and some photographs. Of his parents.

In a way, I was already familiar with the pictures – from his drawings. Time and again he had drawn the whole thing, very precisely, so I must have known. It had been buckshot, you could not help but see it, you had seen it before, but never like this. They lay close together, dressed in evening clothes. They had probably been out and had then come home and had then gone over to him in the camp bed. And he had been lying there, waiting for them.

"Now they'll remember," he said.

He had not looked at the pictures, nor at me. He had looked out of the window, at the moon.

"How come?" I said.

"Now they know I don't put up with anything."

We were running out of time, you had to be clear and forthright.

"They look pretty dead," I said.

"They're perfectly okay," he said, "it was just a reminder."

The typewritten sheets contained the police report, along with the statement from the legal representative from the Department of Health and Welfare, who had to be present whenever you were questioned, if you were under fifteen. I had had that too. There was no time to read those now. That left the papers from Biehl's.

There were a number of letters, from different authorities. I tried to read them, it was no good. We were running late, the cleaners would be here soon and the thing with my hand did not make it any easier. Besides, it was a difficult language to read against the clock. It left you with the same feeling as the standardised reading tests; made you aware of how slow you were. But mostly it was difficult because of August.

He stood beside me looking out of the window. He had seized up. Looking at the papers was like seeing inside him.

But there was something I could not help but notice. Two of the letters were from Baunsbak-Kold, Director of Education for Copenhagen. That was one of the things I saw. The other was what we had come for. It was about August's trial period. I read it several times so as to get it off by heart.

"You're here for an indefinite period," I said, "you're in preventive detention."

I read it out to him, ". . . after consultation with the Department of Health and Welfare, the Ministry of Education, the Danish Institute of Education, the Copenhagen Board of Education and the Danish Teacher Training College, the department hereby assents to August Joon being boarded at the school, under preventive detention, for an indefinite period."

"Why did they ask so many people?" he said. "What was the point of that?"

I did not answer that, there was no time to wonder about it.

"Your trial period won't ever end," I said, "you've got to stick it out. We'll make it, you'll see. We'll think of something."

Then I noticed something else. It looked like an extract from a police record, in August's name. This was not possible, there was no way you could have a record if you were under fifteen. I knew all about that, it was a rule. Then I saw where it was from. It was a transcript from the court records, giving a brief account of August's case.

That should not have been possible. The only people who had access to the court records were the observer from child welfare services and the police, who used them in conjunction with police records. Where no notes could be made against a record – for example with those of us not turned fifteen – we were entered in the court records. As, for example, with all those times you had been brought into a police station for questioning, even though you had never been charged. It was supposed to be strictly confidential. But all the same, there was a transcript about August.

I put the file back. I switched on the light, just for a second, to make sure that he had not dripped on the floor or the rug. Then I saw that one of the desk drawers was fitted with a mortise lock.

This was perfectly normal. Biehl was the head of the school, there had to be a locked drawer in his desk for stamps and maybe small sums of money. There was no good reason for taking a look and besides we were in a hurry.

But I did it anyway. I took a paperclip from the desk and used the sheet-metal key as a wrench. I do not know why I did it, I suppose it was out of habit.

And yet maybe it had not been habit. Maybe it was an attempt to see inside Biehl.

All the papers in the school had been about everything but him. Always. No exceptions. And he had never said a word about himself.

Which was why you read his memoirs. There were four copies in the library, they could be borrowed for a week at a time. They had been out on loan constantly for nine months, even to people who usually did not read anything except what they were given as homework. And yet not even in that had there been one word about him personally.

It was not a deep drawer. In it lay a pile of blank school note-paper. Under the pile were two sheets of the same notepaper, but this time written upon.

I looked over at August. He had sat down, he was very close to falling asleep on the chair. He had already started to twist and turn the way he did when his nightmare was on the way. When I was sure that he could not see anything, I took the two bottom sheets. Then I closed the drawer.

I picked him up, but because of my hand I could do no more than support him. His legs moved, the rest of him was asleep.

5

"WHERE'S TOMORROW?"
This is what she has asked me.

When children cry, you talk to them about tomorrow. If they hurt
themselves and are inconsolable, even though you pick them up,
then you tell them where they are going tomorrow, who they are
going to visit. You move their awareness on a day, away from their
tears. You introduce time into their lives.

The woman has the knack of doing it gently, somehow. Without
promising anything specific, without trying to deny the pain, ten-
derly she draws the child with her into the future. As if to say, we
all have to learn about time. That even so it is possible to grow up
without being damaged.

For my part, I never talk to the child about time. We talk about
other things – though not about anything much – and never about
tomorrow. For me that is impossible. Tomorrow we could all
be wiped out. You think back upon all the promises you did not
manage to keep. Talk about time and you will always end up
making promises. Then it is better to say nothing at all, no matter
what.

And yet, quite often, she comes to me. Seldom to have anything
explained, but often to tell me something.

When she comes over to me, I sit down on the floor. It does not
seem right to tower over her when she is talking to me. Instead I
sit down, then our heads are on a level.

"Where's tomorrow?"

I knew what she meant. She had grasped the concept of changes
in space, that places are different, also from each other. Now time

had been introduced into her life, but she could not grasp it. So she tried to explain it in terms of space, which she had grasped.

Katarina said the same thing, over the telephone, after the total separation. She did most of the talking, because for her there was less risk.

She said she had been thinking about the way you remembered your past. What you remembered, she said, was a string of events and years stretching back from the point where you now found yourself. In other words, a line of time. This might be coloured differently, depending upon what had happened to you. For example, if you had lost someone then it would be black. Other spots might be lighter. On some sections of the line time would have passed quickly, on other sections more slowly. But, for a long way back, it would still be a line.

Though not all the way back – at any rate, not in her case – and what about me? She asked me to think about it.

For her, she said, and maybe for everyone, if you went far enough back the line disintegrated. If you went all the way back to your early childhood it was no longer a line. Then there was a sort of landscape of events. You could not remember their sequence, maybe they had none, they just lay scattered about, as if on a plain. She believed that this plain belonged to the days before time had entered your world.

She asked me to give it some thought.

"Is there any way of asking August," she said, "about what it's like for him, whether there is a plain, or what?"

When I was sitting on the floor facing the child and she asked me about tomorrow, I realised that she was still on the plain, but that she was on the point of stepping into the tunnels where time is to be found.

I so much wanted to understand her, I tried to see whether time showed in her face. But there was nothing I could say to her; no answer I could give her. When I myself did not know where tomorrow was.

"I don't know," I said.

Then I saw that she did not need an answer, that it was not important. What was important was that I had sat on the floor and listened to her.

She stayed where she was. I had the feeling that, whatever I said to her, it would never be that important, that she would never evaluate it or pay too much attention to it. That you could afford to be slow, or inaccurate or downright ignorant without being punished; that still she would stay for a moment, and not walk away.

I asked August how he remembered.

This was one night, a week after I had last been in his room. They looked in on him a few times before lights out, it had taken me a week to work out their schedule. It had proved to be strictly regulated. Flakkedam and the new superintendent took it in turns; they came once every hour, around the hour. That was how I was able to steer clear of them – because they were so regular.

I came just after he had been given his medicine at 21.00, which meant we had until 21.30 when Flakkedam did his round to put out the lights.

He lay on his back looking at the ceiling.

"They've increased the dosage to three Mogadon," he said; "if you've got something to say you'd better hurry."

There was nothing I had to say. I just stood there, looking at him. His skin had a papery look. At the Christian Foundation there had been a reception centre for abandoned babies. They had had incubator babies there – tinier than all the others, but like old men. Very small and yet very old. That was how he looked.

I had taped the two outer fingers together – it hurt least that way. I suppose my little finger should have been in a cast, but then they would have grown suspicious. August pretended not to notice.

He looked feverish. I felt his forehead, keeping one eye on his hands. If anything, he was cold.

"What happens if you stop eating altogether?" he said.

"Two days when you feel hungry," I said, "then two days when it hurts, as though you were ill, after that you feel fine. Until you grow weak and they find out about it and you're forced to eat something."

There had been girls at Nødebogård, and some of them had

127

suffered from an eating disorder. Sometimes, by wearing two sweaters and padding out their stomachs with cushions, they could put off being caught for so long that they only just survived. I did not mention this, there was no point in encouraging him.

He was getting sleepy. He asked me whether I had seen anything of Katarina and I said that she had wanted me to ask him about something. I explained to him about the way in which she believed you remembered your past, how would he say he remembered his?

The same way we did, he said, he too remembered a line, there was nothing strange about that.

I felt a twinge of suspicion.

"Where does it start?" I said. "What's the first thing you remember?"

"The first thing I remember is the office," he said. "I'm in the office and I see you. That's where it starts."

"That's only two and half months ago," I said. "What about before that?"

"There's nothing before that," he said. "Just a black hole."

I did not feel like asking him anything else. I stayed by his side, saying nothing.

He was asleep. His eyes were not quite shut. They were like slits, you could see his pupils, but at the same time you could tell by his breathing that he was asleep. With his eyes half-open. It did not seem right. I placed a finger on each eyelid and gently closed them.

I would have liked to have stayed longer, but it was not possible. Flakkedam could appear at any minute.

He was asleep, I am sure of that, and yet some part of him must have been awake, one of the people inside him. I was by the door when he called me. He whispered.

"If you remember," he said, "and have a past, then you can be given the blame and be punished. See – if you don't remember anything, you don't have time like other people. It's a bit like being crazy, so you get taken into protective custody. Then there's a chance."

The next morning I was summoned to Biehl's office. Fredhøj was there too. They said that, subsequent to the receipt of a reply from the Children's Panel, the school – together with the child welfare services – had come to a decision about my future. Within the next couple of weeks a suitable treatment home would be found for me. This decision was final. They had had it ratified by a judge.

SECOND YEAR SECONDARY – Katarina's class – stood two rows behind our class at Assembly. Fredhøj checked the rows before Biehl came in and began. Although people had their set places, it had always been hard to maintain strict order on the perimeter, where one row bordered on to the next. Those who came in last could not elbow their way through to their proper places; instead they stayed on the perimeter.

Nine days after the total separation, Katarina came in at the last minute, though without actually being late. She managed to stand a little in front of me, almost next to Fredhøj. This blurred their awareness. It would never have occurred to them that she would try anything.

Each pupil brought their own song book to Assembly. Bound editions were compulsory, to save wear and tear. She opened it in such a way that I could not help but see it, but shielded it from everyone but me. The writing was tiny, to reduce the risk of being caught; it took me the whole of Assembly to read it. It said: "What's your guardian's name?"

For all orphans and all children who had been taken into care, whose parents had lost custody of them, a guardian was appointed. It was a rule.

Usually it was a lawyer from the Children's Panel. I had seen mine once. When the Social Welfare committee had given me an indefinite period at Himmelbjerg House she gave me the news. She had told me straight out, that she was appointed as guardian to between two and three hundred children at a time. So, although technically she was my mother and father, there would be no possibility of us meeting again, unless I wanted to get married before I was eighteen, or had a fortune that had to be administered. I had not seen her since.

This was too long-winded an explanation for Katarina. All I wrote in my song book was "Johanna Buhl, Children's Panel". Three days later I moved back a row and held the book up, no one noticed a thing.

The next day I was summoned to the telephone to take a call.

The school had two telephones which were accessible to pupils, both of them located in the annexe – one in the boys' wing and one in the girls'.

Both lines went through the school switchboard in Biehl's secretary's office, but they were pay-phones, you were free to make calls from them and talk on them during the lunch break, from 11.40 to 12.30, and after close of compulsory prep, from 20.15 to 20.50. The call for me came in at 12.05. I was in the playground, a kid from one of the junior classes came to get me. Flakkedam had sent him, he said my guardian was on the phone.

The receiver was lying on the little table for the phone books. It was the first time that anyone had rung me at Biehl's, apart from the two calls from the Health and Welfare representative. Nor had I ever made any calls. The telephone was just fixed to the wall, there was no box. I was glad of that. After the business with Valsang I had not been too keen on small spaces.

It was Katarina.

I had been at the school for a year when the telephones were installed. Before that, getting permission to use the phone had not been easy. The call had to be absolutely necessary, and always had to be made from the school office. You stood there, it was a strain, talking with people walking back and forth. The secretary could hear every word and you knew that you were monopolising the school line. At Assembly Biehl had said that, in principle, telephones were for brief and essential messages only.

Katarina must have rung the school switchboard from the girls' telephone and said she was Johanna Buhl. This was the only possible explanation. She had rung the office from the girls' phone and they had thought it was an outside call and put her through to the boys' side.

A while went by without us saying a single word. We just stood there, holding the receivers. I could hear her breathing – regularly, clearly, almost like a clock. I had not believed I would ever talk to her again, not ever.

"Are you okay?" she said.

"Yes," I said. "But August isn't."

There was no warning, just a click, and we were cut off. Maybe someone had taken her unawares.

She called me again.

The next day, after prep. I picked it up myself. I was standing just beside it when it rang, in a way I had been expecting it.

Since the summer holidays it had been my job to empty the rubbish from the kitchen into the big rubbish bins behind the annexe. This was a much sought-after job. It did not take long and the rubbish bins were kept in a shed, so you could hang around there for a bit, out of sight. I had been given it as a reward for two years without punishment or bad-conduct marks.

After the disaster in the church I had been transferred to odd jobs indoors. No comment was made, but it was a way of keeping me under closer surveillance. It had been a relief. The thing with my fingers had made it difficult to do hard manual work. On the day Katarina rang I had been oiling the door hinges, and had carried on with this after lunch, to be near the telephone.

At the Royal Orphanage there had been a ban on external calls to pupils, unless someone had died or something like that. This was to prevent any weakening of the moral fibre which the school was at pains to develop.

So people were only called to the telephone when there was something seriously amiss in their families. Or when the social services department or the police wanted to speak to them – which was worse.

You had, therefore, got used to the telephone playing its part in the surveillance of pupils. And to its being used only by teachers and the school management.

Suddenly – standing there with the receiver in my hand and Katarina on the other end – it was different, almost the opposite.

Usually there was a queue of people, this day there was no one. It rang, and I picked it up before anyone could hear it.

She was out of breath. She must have waited until no one was in sight, and then made a dash for it. She had been working in the garden all through the autumn, so they must have moved her indoors too.

Again it struck me that her breathing was like a clock, that it marked off this short time when we could be together.

We said nothing. We just stood there, leaning into the sound of each other's breathing.

That was when she told me how you remembered in a line that ended a long way back in a plain. Every now and then the pips went and she put in more money. Where had she got that?

"Can we meet?" she said.

I had thought this all the way through to the end, in case she should ask. There was only one way, I said, and that was at night. I could help her out of the window and down, could she manage that?

"They've moved me," she said. "I'm sleeping in the same room as the new superintendent."

She had said it quite quietly, and yet it was as though something big, like a train, had come racing along and then passed by, and with the train had gone the last chance of seeing her.

"I'm going away in two weeks," I said. "To a treatment home."

The receiver was put down. There was no sound, as there had been last time. One minute we were connected, the next we were cut off.

I stayed by the telephone for a while, but nothing happened.

7

TWO DAYS IN A ROW I spent the lunch break in the library.

Under different circumstances I would have been banned, but the school's rhythm was altered, because of the snow.

The snow had fallen gently, but it had fallen day and night, and they had not been able to keep pace with it. Andersen shovelled snow and gritted and salted, helped by those boarders on outdoor chores. The playground was a sheet of ice and there were great mounds of snow. This meant that the little ones were allowed to stay upstairs, people took longer to come into class because of their wet clothes and, all in all, you sensed a deviation from the timetable.

Both Fredhøj and Karin Ærø saw me in the library, but nothing was said. Maybe they thought I had already been punished; that no more could be done to me.

I looked through old numbers of the blue book, the school year-book. Each volume contained a picture of every class. I looked at the old photographs of her class – from when she started in Primary I and all the way up.

These days I saw her at Assembly too. It hurt to look straight at her, it was easier with pictures.

In those days the girls had worn pigtails, and so did she. Otherwise she looked just the same.

Apart from the fact that she was smiling. There were eight pictures, from 1963 to 1971. In 1970 she was missing. The school photographs were taken in April, which was when she had been absent. In the first seven pictures she was smiling. Not much, but nevertheless it was noticeable. So it was clear to see the kind of home she came from, and what life had been like for her. Then you could see why she had talked about a light plain.

Then came the year when she was missing. And then came the

last picture, from this year. In which she was not smiling. And her clothes were different. You could only see her top half, but she was wearing one of the big sweaters.

I laid the books end to end, to see all of them at once. Like a line of time.

You could not get the thought out of your head: what if you had known her back then, what would it have been like? Maybe you could have seen something of one another, she might have invited me home, I might have met her parents, and when disaster started to strike I could have helped her.

That is what I thought, that I could have helped her. I, who had never even been able to help myself.

I looked at the pictures. Eventually it seemed as though you had grown up with her. As though you had not shot up feverishly only after coming to Biehl's, but had always been there and had grown up with her, quietly and peacefully, so that now you belonged together.

Before this I had never looked much at photographs. You would have thought that they would have changed when you turned upon them the light of awareness. That they would become weaker, like the fear. This was not the case. Instead they became deeper and deeper. I sat there and looked at them for two days in a row. I would have gone up there on the third day too, if it had not started to snow again, and we had been sent for a run.

$$\bigcirc\!\!\!8$$

THE NEXT BEST THING – after apparatus work – for strengthening the front was athletics, especially the field events although, since these were outdoor sports, it was more difficult to practise them in the winter.

The only exception was running. Klastersen had taught the junior national team to take winter training runs across the frozen marshes and lakes, and had achieved fine results. It was one of his ground rules – running was something that could be done in all weathers.

So all year round you went for training runs, although he had a marked preference for snow. Then it was a pretty safe bet that you would have to run round the grounds, at least for the first half-hour.

Klastersen himself ran at the head. This meant that if you did not keep up with the leaders, or if you actually let yourself fall behind, then suddenly you found yourself on your own.

She was standing beside a tree, with her back turned. I saw the black coat. The falling snow formed a wall behind her. She broke away from the tree, stepped through the wall and was gone.

I turned off the path and came down to the lake. There was one spot on it that always took a lot longer to freeze over. A heron was standing there, and there were swans too. They seemed not to feel the cold, they were flapping about as though someone had passed that way.

I thought I had lost her, or maybe it had not been her. The snow kept on forming chambers, you ran through never-ending rows of white rooms. I turned up towards the hill with the statues – icy suits of snow over bronze-green skin. One of them broke loose and moved off. I started walking. At the spot where we came down, in

136

the summer, there had been roses. They had been cut back and covered with fir branches, she had helped with that, I had seen her there not long after I had written the letter. Now everything was covered with snow; just four mounds forming one long, white trench.

She broke into a run, but did not get far. The snow was deep and she was only wearing thin shoes. She kind of crumpled up and hunkered down. I came up behind her. She half-turned her face towards me.

"Go away," she said, "get lost!"

She must have shouted, but the snow absorbed the sound. I had seen half of her face. There was hate in it.

I stayed put, I had nothing to lose. I had nothing to put round her, I had been running in just a sweatshirt. I understood none of this.

She got up and started walking. I followed. We came down to the lake, the snow and the water ran into one another, no sign of any downward movement, just a grey wave between heaven and earth. You were enclosed, as in a cell or a white hospital. And yet you were free, on all sides you were hidden from view.

She did not turn her head, I had to lean towards her to catch the words.

"Just go," she said. "Go to hell."

"I've been transferred," I said. "It's a punishment, they've had it ratified by a judge, there's nothing to done."

She turned her face towards me, the skin was white, transparent. She looked at me as though she were searching for something. Then she touched my arm.

"They're having you transferred?"

She kept her eyes fixed on me, it was almost overwhelming.

"I was waiting for you," she said. "I have the timetable, I knew you would come."

We walked along side by side, we had run out of options. But it did not matter. She stumbled, I took her arm. We were in a desolate forest, I had protected her, I had wrapped extra blankets around her. It was getting darker, we were heading into the darkness, towards destruction, but it did not matter.

You spend your whole life believing that you will always be on the outside or on the borderline. You struggle and struggle, and yet it all seems to be in vain. And then, suddenly, you are allowed inside and lifted up into the light.

She looked at me, there was snow on her eyelashes and flakes of ice – tears, she was crying, and not out of hostility, and not because I had hit her. It was the first time in my life.

"I thought you wanted to leave," she said.

I wanted to ask for permission to kiss her, but I could not speak, I tried but I could not. And yet maybe I did say it, because it happened. Her lips were chapped with the cold.

It was everything, that kiss was everything. Everything you had dreamed of but never attained, and everything that, now, would never come to pass, because I was going away and was lost. All of that was in it.

It got rid of time. I knew I would remember it for ever and ever and that they could not take it away from me, not ever – come what may. And so that moment became one of utter fearlessness.

A house came at us out of the darkness. That is how it seemed, even though it was we who were moving. It was one of the storehouses. It was locked, but only by a padlock with a shackle. You loosen the nut and the shackle pin slips down.

There had been a bit about the storehouses in Biehl's memoirs. When the school, achieving a significant goal, had added school-leaving certificate classes to the curriculum, it had been necessary to move some of the school's collections – which were valuable but stored away – out of the main building. In time it was hoped that they would form the nucleus of a museum to the Grundtvigian educational tradition.

There was no light. There were boxes and gardening tools on the floor; along the walls – glass-fronted cabinets. Darkness was falling outside, but behind the glass I saw Magdeburg hemispheres, glass retorts and a Van de Graaff generator. Along with a large number of stuffed birds, and a civet caught in the coils of a cobra.

The snake was bigger than the civet, it had a good grip and was starting to squeeze. At the same time it had stretched its jaws wide and exposed its poisonous fangs. The animals were frozen in the moment just before the strike.

I knew that the civet would win. It was not something I wanted to happen, it was something I knew would happen. It had most to lose, its life was on the line – and maybe the lives of others, whom it was protecting from the snake – and it was the smaller, and it had its back to the wall. It was a little, restless, wild animal and the snake was bigger, cold and steady. Even so, it did not stand a chance.

We sat down on a couple of boxes.

"What are we going to do?" she said.

A moment before you could not have imagined that there was anything you could do. Now things had changed, now we would have to leave the school. That was easily arranged, I wanted to explain it to her. There had been people who had run away from Himmelbjerg House, and who had stayed out, on the loose, for up to two weeks and more. And here the situation was different, together we could stay out for ever.

These were the words I wanted to say. Instead I said something else.

"August," I said.

Never, ever, can you abandon a child without crashing into perdition yourself. It is a rule against which one personally can do nothing.

She had known this, before I said it she had known. It had never been just us two, never just Katarina and me. There had always been three of us, even before he came and I saw him for the first time.

I told her about the service corridors and about his dossier. I did not say much, nor was it necessary. She sat on the box, leaning forwards, and listened to me, even to my pauses. She heard everything, even the things I could not say.

We sat there and I knew that this was how it felt to be totally accepted. You sit close to another person and are understood, everything is understood and nothing is judged and you are indispensable.

And we sat on, saying nothing. I tried to find a solution, to find out how to get August out, so that we could be together, all three of us. The locks were there, before my eyes – first those between him and us – on the main door and the corridor and the sickbay, and the lock of the cupboard where they kept his outdoor clothes and shoes at night. And then, once we had got to him, the locks between us and freedom – on the car we would have to use, and in front of the money you had to have. And beyond them, all the locks in the world, a never-ending host. No one could open that many. It would be an overwhelming achievement, one that would never come to an end, no matter how much you struggled and did your best.

It became obvious that we were lost, and then came the despair.

Although only for August, not for Katarina and definitely not for me. I had been given everything and no one could ever take that away from me. For someone who has been given everything you cannot feel despair.

I was sure that Katarina had been thinking the same. That, in that moment, we were thinking the same thought, without having to discuss it. I was convinced of that.

Then she stood up and went over to the window, and just by the way she walked I could see that I had been wrong.

"If there were no clocks in the school," she said, "what would you know about time?"

Her voice had changed, she was in another world, she was another person. Inside her, at the same time, there was another person – but a different person – who had now taken over.

It was like August, and yet not the same. August was either the one person or the other, there was no connection. The August who stood with his back to the wall and went for your fingers was out of control.

With Katarina it was different. The two people were connected, they were both there at the same time, but this one, the one that had now taken over, I would never understand.

I could have gone on sitting with her for all time. That is how it was, and that is how it will be for the rest of my life. If the child, August, had also been there, I could have sat there with the woman always.

I never wanted anything else. Nor have I, since then. Than to be allowed inside, and then to sit quietly with the woman and the child. That would have been enough.

But now I saw that it was different for Katarina. And that she, and maybe every person, was like row upon row of white rooms.

You can go together through some of them, but they have no end, and you cannot accompany anyone through them all.

I would never have got her to come with me. Not even if we could have brought August. The other part of her, some of the other people inside her, wanted something more. They wanted an answer.

In the laboratory she had asked a question: what was time, what was the plan behind the school? – and as yet the question had not been answered.

It is not easy to understand. That it can be so important for someone to ask a question and receive an answer; that it is more important than anything else. Maybe even more important than love.

There is no way you can understand it. You have to give in and say: that is how it is. That they need to know. No matter what.

She asked again.

"What would you know about time if there were no clocks?"

I suppose you'd still be aware of it, I said, and we'd better be getting back soon. It was almost dark, I had seen Klastersen outside, he must have realised that I was missing, and made one more circuit.

I thought of her breathing on the telephone, and breathing in general.

"You breathe," I said, "and there's your heartbeat, it's like a clock. The sun and the moon rise and set."

"Those are rhythms," she said, "there's some kind of order, there's no confusion. But it isn't total regularity."

I had no answer to that. Klastersen had run off into the darkness.

"Tell me again, about the letters," she said. "The bit about the Director of Education."

She had moved up close to me, I took my time telling her. I could no longer see her face.

She took my arm.

"I brought you a watch," she said.

She put it on my wrist. Where had she got that?

"Now, listen," she said.

And then she explained something to me.

141

AT THE BEGINNING of January 1993, I cycled all over Copenhagen looking for a particular clock.

By then I had been writing the account here presented for over a year, and I had kept putting off this one task: after twenty years, once more having to enter a school.

It was cold and very dark. It was daytime, but still murky enough for night.

I started at random with Øster Farimagsgade School, maybe because from the hill in the grounds around Biehl's you could always see the tower of the church next to it.

The school office was on a mezzanine floor. I stood for a long while in front of the secretaries, then I pulled myself together, "Might I be allowed to see your school bell?" I said. "I'm writing a book."

It was high up, encapsulated in Plexiglas and sporting red digital figures. They told me that it had been installed before their time – no one could remember when – and kept perfect time. Very occasionally a man came to give it a once-over.

A teacher came by while I was standing there. Five years earlier he had been working at Frederiksundsvejen's School, he thought they had an old bell there.

So I cycled out to Frederiksundsvej. They had the same Plexiglas box and digital display. But they gave me the telephone number of the school engineer.

I managed to speak to him a few days later. He was employed by the District Engineer's office, with responsibility for timekeeping in many of the schools in Copenhagen District. He told me that, over the past twenty years, a private company, Danish Time Management Ltd, had been given the job of replacing most of the old bells with modern, quartz mechanisms. Which were very accurate, and required hardly any adjusting. And so, to all intents and purposes, ran all by themselves. Without any human intervention.

He did, however, know of two old-style mechanisms. Hellig Kor's School and Prinsesse Charlotte's Gade School still had the old-style bells. The kind that had been in use in the '60s and '70s. But which time had made obsolete.

I cycled to Hellig Kor's School, and there I came very close. The clock was in the office. It was the right casing, but there were too many wires. They told me that the works had been replaced, some years earlier, by an electronic mechanism.

I found it at Prinsesse Charlotte's Gade School.

The deputy headmaster came with me. I felt very small. To me he seemed a generation older. Later on it dawned on me that he and I must have been just about of an age.

The clock was high up. He held the ladder for me.

This was the clock I had been searching for. The clock I had seen and touched just once, for an instant, one forenoon twenty-two years before. A hand-wound Bürk pendulum clock.

I opened the glass and took a look at the works. I meant to take a few notes, but there was no need. It was just as I remembered.

The deputy head, the engineer, the secretaries in the office, the teacher who had worked at Frederiksundsvejen's School – all of them have forgotten me within no time of having met me. But, while we were standing together, they thought they were dealing with an adult.

Wrong. They had been speaking to a child.

Confronted by them I had no skin, nothing to shield me. I noted their every change in tone, every shift of the eye; I sensed their need to be getting on, their politeness and distraction and indifference. They forgot me five minutes after I was gone, I will remember them always.

Crossing the threshold of a school, I stepped inwards and downwards into the child I was twenty-two years ago, and in this form I met the adults.

They were protected. Time had wrapped a membrane around

143

them. They were jovial and pressed for time and totally unaffected by our meeting.

That is how it was then, when I was at Biehl's. That is how it is now, that is how it will always be. Time has wrapped itself around the adults – with its haste, its dread, its ambition, its bitterness and its long-term goals. They no longer see us properly and what they do see they have forgotten five minutes later.

While we, we have no skin. And we remember them always.

That is how it was at the school. We remembered every facial expression, every insult and word of encouragement, every casual remark, every expression of power and weakness. To them we were everyday, to us they were timeless, cosmic, and overwhelmingly powerful.

This thought has crossed my mind: that when you feel pain, when you feel that this thing growing, here, in the laboratory, is all for nothing, you could counteract it with the thought that now this is perhaps the only way of telling how the world seemed to you back then.

Things adult. Precise, accurate things. Of those there is no shortage. In fact, everything else around us is comprised of them. But to sense without skin is something that can perhaps only be done under conditions such as those in the laboratory.

$$\left(\begin{array}{c} 10 \end{array}\right)$$

I DID NOT let myself into August's room. I could not risk getting caught. Instead I went up to the door and called to him, it was just before he was due to have his medicine. We lay down and talked through the gap at the bottom of the door. Which meant that I could not see him and I could only just hear him. I said no more than was absolutely vital – that I was going to report him for having gone without eating for a long time.

"It'll mean Sandbjerggård," he said; "they've got a clinic there, then it's all over."

"No," I said. "You'll be admitted to the infirmary, on a yellow slip, or a red one. It's all worked out."

The infirmary was on the fifth floor, diagonally opposite the assembly hall, beside the district medical officer's clinic. It was bigger than the sickbay, with two beds instead of just an examining table, and a locked cupboard for instruments.

The sickbay was for people suffering from minor ailments or those who had to be kept in isolation for a while. The infirmary was for real accidents.

After Axel Fredhøj's second accident he was taken there, while they waited for the ambulance. And Werner Petersen, who had been the PE teacher before Klastersen, was taken there too. He had always been tough and yet, at the same time, nervous. He had never been able to cope with people leaving a room before he did, a strict ban had been in force against leaving the gym during his classes. Which was not easy, since the place was not heated in winter and you could easily find yourself needing to go to the toilet, which was why one day Kåre Frymand had peed in the wastepaper basket in the changing room. It was done out of desperation and with the best of intentions, not to have to go all the way up to the toilets. He was very scared of Werner Petersen. Being wicker the waste-paper basket was not watertight. It leaked and Werner Petersen set about punishing him. You had sensed that this was not like the other times, he went off his head and screamed like a madman. Someone had gone to get other teachers who had overpowered him and locked him up in the infirmary. It had been done on the quiet, the rest of the school would never have found out about it if Kåre Frymand had not sustained some damage and an explanation been demanded of the school. It was said that it was a breakdown. There were special circumstances surrounding Werner Petersen's family for some time, and he never returned to the school. Klastersen was appointed in his place.

From then on it was obvious what the infirmary was used for. Because it was close to the staff room and the office and had direct access to the south stairs it was ideal for things that were not to be bandied about.

Never before had I heard of anyone at Biehl's suffering from an eating disorder. But at the Royal Orphanage and especially at Himmelbjerg House it had been common. The management there knew that it was not dangerous if people were caught in time. Even so, they had not wanted it discussed. People were put to bed and the doctor was called and an admittance slip was filled out – yellow if they were only a danger to themselves, red if they were also a danger to their surroundings. This was a strictly regulated pro-cedure, I had explained this to Katarina in the storehouse.

There was no time, nor any chance, to tell August this. I hoped it would work the same way here at the school – that was our plan. Although I could not be sure. But, in any case, neither August nor I had more than a few days left. I mean, we had come to the point where there really was not much to discuss.

"I can't stay on my own at night," he said.

I comforted him by saying that they would have someone watch-ing him.

"It'll be Flakkedam," he said.

You knew what he meant. That that was worse than being alone.

"Don't swallow the medicine," I said.

I would have told him just to swallow the tablets, so there would

146

be nothing to feel when Flakkedam checked, but not to drink the water afterwards. When Flakkedam had gone he could stick his finger down his throat and they would come up.

I had no chance to explain this. He had started making noises, like an animal, then everything went quiet.

"It's a conspiracy," he said, "you're in it too."

I could hear him dragging himself away from the gap. I placed my lips right down against the floor.

"One night," I said, "two at the most."

He was moving away.

"We won't go without you," I said.

I reported him to Flakkedam that same evening. I said it straight out: he had not eaten in two weeks, he had just pretended to eat at suppertime, I just thought I ought to let them know, to protect a schoolfriend, so that something could be done about it.

Flakkedam wasted no time in calling down Biehl. I saw them going into the sickbay, then they carried August straight across to the main building, you could see them going up the stairs, it did not look as though August offered any resistance. Not long afterwards a car drove up and parked in the south playground. You heard it, you did not see it – but it was not an ambulance. I guessed it must be the district medical officer.

I did not sleep that night.

$$\cdot 11 \cdot$$

AT HIMMELBJERG HOUSE, the second time I refused to run away, the others made me drink Solignum, which was a wood preservative used for creosoting the outhouses and so readily available. It contained various fungicides, so I had soon become unwell and the management had found out about it. They had wanted to contain it within the school walls. They would have pumped my stomach, but there was no equipment for this, so instead the nurse gave me copper sulphate. No explanation was given, it was just a matter of getting it down. This and the effect I had remembered.

Blue crystals, that was copper sulphate. I took about a spoonful from the art-room cupboard, while Karin Ærø was in the room, but with her back turned.

The cupboard held various chemicals, fixer spray, benzine, refill bottles of ink – and copper sulphate. It was used, along with salt crystals, in silk painting to get the paint to form patterns. I had seen it and recognised it long before, but had not given it a second thought.

Although the cupboard was usually locked, during class it was left open. No one saw me, even though the room was full of people. You could well understand why. When I put in my hand and opened the little jar I sensed that both the time and the place were so far out of bounds, so far beyond imagining, that I became as if invisible.

Later on in the period I also took a white coat from the cupboard. It was one of Karin Ærø's, it was a bit paint-spattered. This was not difficult either. She did not seem to see me. Everyone knew I would be leaving and so, in a way, I had ceased to exist.

*   *   *

What I had to do needed to take place during Fredhøj's class, double physics.

When it came to the pupils, Fredhøj had insight. Biehl was in all ways greater, but Fredhøj was more dangerous. Because he was as quiet and jovial and intelligent as though he were on the pupils' side. And yet still saw and understood everything. He was deadly.

Faced with any other teacher you could have come up with an excuse or made a show of feeling sick and been permitted to leave the room. With Fredhøj this was impossible.

He is dead now, he died some years ago. He had already been dead for some time when I heard about it. They said it was a stroke.

In a way you knew it had to have been. You had always sensed that there was some kind of enormous pressure inside him.

For me he lives on. Often he has come to me, in the laboratory, when I have been sitting there, writing. On these occasions he is always kindly, accurate, amusing, impeccably dressed and wise.

Then you feel like bowing down to him, and thanking him for what he gave to you, for the book-learning and the humour and something else, something confidence-inspiring. And I have done it. I have bowed down to him and thanked him and remembered his kindness.

And then the fear has come.

Against those people who are open and distinct you have a chance of protecting yourself. Biehl for example, or Karin Ærø – for them you could feel pure fear.

With Fredhøj it was more difficult, if not impossible. He radiated kindness. This caused you somehow to draw near and lean towards him. It seemed like he wanted to protect you, so – even though you knew better – you leaned forwards.

Then you sensed that something was dreadfully wrong.

Five minutes before the class, I swallowed the copper sulphate. The timing was very important. When I put it in my mouth my body remembered it and did not want it, but I forced it down.

149

Twenty minutes later it took effect. Much later, therefore, than the first time. The reaction was violent, under any other circumstances you would have been shaken, but now I had experience.

This was not your usual vomiting, there was no steadily building nausea. It was like a sudden attack, everything swam in front of your eyes and you broke into a cold sweat. Fredhøj spotted me straight away, I could tell by his face how bad I must look and that he entertained no suspicions. Then my stomach contracted five or six times in rapid succession and threw up its entire contents. I made it to the washbasin, there was nothing to mop up.

With that, it was all over. I knew from the time before that I would now be weak but otherwise perfectly alright.

But I still did not look well, Fredhøj had the monitor see me to my room. When we were down on the stairs I sent her back. Then I put on Katarina's watch and ascended to the fifth floor.

The door to the infirmary was not locked. August was lying in the bed nearest the door, with a duvet over him. I took it off, they had him strapped down. He was so thin, I had never seen anything like it. Apart from that, everything was as you would expect, the anorexic girls at Nødebogård had been given the same treatment: two drips, saline solution and glucose, and a tube down the nose for force-feeding. Besides the straps across arms and chest they had also bound one across his forehead to stop him from shaking out the tube. He was very far away, they must have given him something strong to make him sleep.

His eyes were half-open, but he was asleep. I closed his eyelids and, even though he could not hear me, I whispered to him that he was to take it very easy. Then I had to leave him, there was no more time.

There was a little window in the office door. I jumped up, even though I was weak from the copper sulphate, the office was empty. I tried the door: it was locked, but it was a standard one-lever Chubb.

I positioned myself outside Biehl's office, I had no idea whether he was in there or not.

Katarina's directions had been as follows: the phone would ring between twenty-five past and half-past. At that time the office would be closed, the secretary would be at Queen Caroline Amalie's

Charity Schools Foundation, where she had meetings every Wednesday and Thursday. The foundation paid a proportion of the school's running costs and had also donated the new Challenge Cup. When the phone rang I was to let myself in and put whoever was calling through to the pupils' telephone in the girls' wing.

Until then I was to wait in the corridor.

This was Katarina's plan. She did not know any better, she herself had never done much waiting about on the fifth floor.

Because the staff room was at the end of the corridor, people were constantly coming and going. Besides which, August was now in the infirmary, there was bound to be someone watching him, probably the school nurse or Flakkedam. There were bound to be regular checks. I had no lawful business in the corridor and was very exposed. I would be seen and an explanation demanded of me.

So I put myself outside Biehl's office, it was the worst possible place, but it was the only thing to do. I stood up straight so as not to touch the wall, with my hands behind my back and my head bowed. Quite a few teachers came past, I did not look up at them, they did not stop. They assumed that I was waiting to see Biehl, to be punished.

The phone never rang. I stayed there until twenty-five to, and even a bit longer. Then it was necessary to leave, or else I would get caught in the stream of teachers who would turn up when the lunch bell rang.

Going down the stairs I saw Flakkedam.

To be on the safe side, I peered down through the shaft formed by the banisters. I saw his hand, far below. I managed to let myself in to the third floor and positioned myself in the weaving room until he had passed.

Maybe he was on his way up to check on August. I had only seen one of his hands, that was enough to identify him. Although there was something different, the two outer fingers were in plaster. So, in spite of everything, they must have lost control of August for an instant.

I did not sleep that night either. Because of the copper sulphate it had not been possible to eat anything. All night long I sat, looking

151

out over the grounds and across at the school, thinking of August. Whether I should go over to him, and remove the tubes and the straps and sit with him so that he could see we had not forgotten him and then he could sleep. But it had been snowing, Flakkedam would have seen the tracks and it would have been the end of everything.

I would have gone anyway. If I had not been stopped by what Katarina had said.

I had not seen her since she told me about the plan, in the store-house. Not so much as a glimpse. But before we split up she had given me the watch and had herself fastened the strap round my wrist. Then she had held on to me and looked straight at me through the darkness and then she had said: "Twice, we'll try twice."

The darkness began to close in, then the thought struck that everything we were doing was for nothing, then I came close to giving up.

I wanted to go home.

At Himmelbjerg House and Crusty House the set-up in the showers had been the same: three showers in a row – the first was warm, the last two were cold. You lined up, soaped yourself at the washbasins and then passed through the showers, pretty fast. There was a window in the wall. That was where Valsang stood, where he could both keep an eye on you and stay dry.

But occasionally you might be last in line and the others would have gone off. Then you could just stand under the hot water. And that was like coming home.

Now I sat in the dark and wished for that. I purposely avoided the thought of Katarina and August. If I had not been weak I would have tried to get into the showers. I thought that since nothing had been of any use anyway, then it might have helped to stand under the warm water, just like at Crusty House, and sense your own body, even your groin, totally without even a hint of cramp, and let go of time and give up.

At one point, in the morning, the light began to grow. It did not come from any particular spot, it spread out from the surface of things, on the trees and the stonework of the school – like a coating, still very faint, but clear nevertheless. Like a passive resistance against the dark.

Then, too, came Oscar Humlum.

He swung himself in through the window, still on the same rope as back then, and jumped down on to the floor, heavily agile.

"How come you're here?" I said.

He did not answer, so then I said it for him, the way he had always wanted me to do. In spite of everything, I was better with words than he was.

"It's because time has been put on hold," I said.

I could tell by looking at him that this was the case.

He placed himself a little behind me, together we looked out at the light, then I remembered something that had long been forgotten.

We were going to shower. We were last. Valsang was standing on his side of the window. Humlum went in ahead of me. He walked straight through the warm shower as though it did not exist and in under the first of the cold ones. And there he stayed. He did not move, he just stood there, while his skin went first red and then white. He looked at his feet, I knew he stayed there so that I could stay in the warm shower and not be made to get a move on. I had shut my eyes, the warm water closed up, like a wall. I had never stood for as long before.

I looked at Humlum. He was standing in the semi-darkness, looking at his feet, as he had done back then. I could not help but think of August in the sickbay and of Katarina lying next to the new superintendent, and then it was not possible to give up and just let things slide. Back then, too, I had eventually pushed him on and gone into the first and then the second cold shower and then out.

12

THE PHONE RANG at half-past precisely. The secretary was in the office at the time, disaster came close.

We had had Fredhøj again from 10.50 to 11.40. That is, at the time when, according to the plan, I was supposed to leave the class. It was unfortunate, but unavoidable, science subjects took up more of the timetable than anything else.

But luck was on my side. Because I had neither eaten nor slept and still bore the mark of the copper sulphate, I looked pretty ill. When I went up to Fredhøj and told him straight that I was feeling unwell, he let me go.

"This is the second day in a row," he said. "I'll have a word with you after class."

There would not be any "after class", I thought. Even though it was not clear what would happen, after class school time would no longer exist.

I ascended to the fifth floor, I did not see a soul. I walked past the infirmary without looking in.

The office door was open. From inside, I could hear the secretary talking.

The plan had not anticipated this. Katarina had pointed to the timetable. "On Wednesdays and Thursdays, between 11.00 and 12.00, she's out."

At first I stopped dead. You had got used to the school timetable being infallible. In all my time, changes had hardly ever been made to classes. Faced with an alteration you became helpless.

So I went into the infirmary. I still had a few minutes. August was lying asleep, but this time I had to wake him. I shook him very hard, he woke up pretty fast. Because of the tube up his nose he could not speak.

"I've come," I said, "you'll need to help me."

There was no time to explain. I loosened one of his hands and passed him a bottle for peeing into.

"The phone's going to ring in a minute," I said. "Count to three slowly, then make some noise, but not too much."

I stepped into the corridor at half-past precisely. There was not a soul in sight. We were moving along narrow tunnels in time and space that only existed at this moment. In a few minutes the bell would ring and people would come out and everything would collapse. But just at this moment we had created a space for ourselves in the stream of time – in between the seconds.

Then the telephone rang. I entered the office.

"Biehl's Academy," she said.

"I think he's choking," I said.

The secretary had been at the school for some years, it was said that she was a distant relation of Biehl. Under other circumstances she would have finished the telephone conversation and not forgotten herself in front of a pupil, but things were different now. Everything at the school was a bit out of joint, everyone had the feeling that something was up. She heard me and stopped short.

At that moment there was a sound from the infirmary, he had thrown the bottle on the floor. It sounded alarming, without being too loud. Quite precisely administered.

I sensed her panic. Although she was self-possessed enough to say, "One moment," into the receiver. Then she ran out.

I picked up the phone, it was a man.

"Put me through to Hessen," he said.

Katarina had described the switchboard to me. It was to the left of the desk. She had said that everything was quite clearly marked, so you did not have to think, and she was right. If you had had to think I would have been lost.

There were three incoming lines. I had no idea which one he was on so I pulled out all three. At the third pull he was cut off, so I stuck that plug into the socket marked "Pupil Telephone". Katarina had said that it would ring automatically, and that I was to listen in over the headphones. Although she had not anticipated that I would have the secretary just outside the door.

I heard the telephone ring, I heard it being picked up. Then someone said, "School psychologist's clinic."

It was Katarina's voice.

"Baunsbak-Kold," he said. "Is Hessen there?"

She answered as though she had not heard the question.

"As we have already stated," she said, "we have a serious problem. We would like you to come over at once."

"That is quite out of the question," he said.

"It's about August Joon, as we said, there's violence."

"Let me speak to Hessen," he said.

I remembered him from the presentation at Gladsaxe Stadium, he had had a chauffeur-driven car. Well-dressed and brilliant. He might have been sitting in the office.

What made it worse was that I could hear something else. I had my back to Biehl's office door. I heard Biehl's voice coming from there. According to the plan he should not have been there but, nevertheless, there he was.

Now I was very exposed, caught between the secretary and Biehl and the Director of Education.

"We can no longer be held responsible," said Katarina. "It's all starting to fall apart."

He had asked for Hessen, and she had not given him an answer. It was Katarina's voice, and yet it was not her. One of the people living inside her, whom I would never understand, had taken over.

I could hear his breathing.

"I'm on my way," he said. "Put me through to the office."

I moved the plug back to where it had come from.

"Office," I said.

"Let me talk to Biehl."

He would not take her word for it. Now he wanted confirmation.

"He's been called away," I said. "There's been an accident."

I could hear the secretary running along the corridor. I replaced the receiver. She came through the door.

"He's not well," she said, "we have to get hold of Flakkedam."

156

"I'm just on my way down to him," I said. "I'll ask him to come up immediately."

She had not really heard me.

"He's so thin," she said.

13

THERE COULD BE no thought now of returning to the class or the annexe. Fredhøj had wanted a word with me, was possibly looking for me. There was nowhere left in the school where I could stay for any length of time and feel safe. I took to the landing between the ground and first floors, across from the junior classes. From here I would be able to see if a teacher came along, and be able to run for cover. When the bell rang for the lunch break I mingled with the stream and let myself be carried out into the playground. Flage Biehl was on playground duty, but he did not seem to have been alerted. At one point Fredhøj appeared under the archway, but I ducked down and next time I looked he was gone. When all the pupils were assembled there were so many, all looking so alike that it was difficult to pinpoint one in particular.

But I saw Katarina. While Flage was at the other end we both made for the centre line. We walked side by side, from the wall to the school, with the line between us and without looking at one another.

"He could be here any time now," she said. "When the bell rings, you've got to go around to the south playground and meet him, instead of going to class."

"They'll be looking for me," I said. "You too."

"Not until the end of the period."

"There isn't enough time," I said.

Around us they were playing two-man tag. An uneven layer of ice covered the tarmac. You ran hand in hand, always a boy and a girl together. The ice made it hard to keep a hold of one another, so you had to take off your mittens. Which meant that you held a girl by the hand. With no mittens in between. Then too, the sense of disintegration was intensified by the fact that Christmas was coming.

We watched them playing. Not long ago we had been of their number but now, suddenly, they were remote from us. It was not just because you had been expelled and would soon be going away, and so need not think any more about them. It was something else. It was Katarina, and that I had kissed her, and August, and that we were on the point of having understood, and that there was no way back.

"There's something I want to ask you," she said. "Can you put back the school clock, the one that controls the bell?"

At the Orphanage, classes were called in and let out by the ringing of a little handbell. It hung from the roof of a shed next to the school building. For boarders' mealtimes and bedtimes there had been a bigger bell out in front of the cloakroom, both bells were a gift from the royal family. The job of bell-ringer was the most sought-after in the school and only ever entrusted to a senior who had achieved something outstanding.

Never during the time I was there had anyone other than the bell-ringer ever laid a finger on the bells. But, since they hung where they were readily accessible, the punishment for their unauthorised ringing had nevertheless been officially determined – instant expulsion.

There was no such punishment at Biehl's. You had seen the bells but never the clock itself. There was never any idea that it might be possible to get close to it. Before Katarina mentioned it, it had never occurred to me, nor to anyone else.

"The clock is not in Biehl's office," she said. "And it's not in the school office either. It has to be in the staff room or behind that door between the infirmary and Fredhøj's office."

"It could be in Andersen's house," I said.

She shook her head.

"It's too important," she said. "It would never be at ground level. It'll be kept up in the light. Close to Biehl and Fredhøj."

I said nothing, I had not answered her. Nor did she seem to expect me to. It was all over. But, for these final moments, we were in the laboratory and anything was possible.

She turned towards me. Then she stepped over the line and came right up close to me.

"Put it back ten minutes," she said. "That will give us the time we need. And something will happen, there's going to be chaos of some sort. And ten minutes is not too much. It will be quite precisely administered."

We walked through the gym together and round to the south stairway, shortly before the bell rang, so as not to be seen by the teacher on playground duty. When we split up she touched my arm.

The Director of Education arrived just after the bell had rung. He was driving himself, he did not so much as look at me.

I walked ahead of him up the stairs and opened the door into the clinic. Katarina was sitting behind the desk, where Hessen usually sat.

"Where's Biehl?" he said.

She did not answer him right away. She stood up and put her hand out to him, he had to take it.

"Katarina," she said. "I'm Hessen's assistant."

At that moment I saw her clothes in a new light. She was wearing a baggy grey sweater. At this moment, behind the desk, she looked like someone older.

I did not hear what he said next. I went out on to the landing and closed the door behind me.

There were panes of glass in the door from the stairs to the fifth floor. I stayed where I was until the corridor was empty, then I went for August. He was very far away, I undid the straps and got him out on to the floor, he kept collapsing, I slapped him several times. He half-opened his eyes, it would have to do, our time was almost up.

It was not clear how he should be presented, but I had a notion that it should be the same as for the school doctor – in other words, everything off except his underpants. They had given him a hospital vest that buttoned up the front and long socks – I took them off.

It occurred to me that the tubes and bottles hooked up to him might be advantageous, so I let him keep them – the ones hanging from needles as well as the ones up his nose and down his throat. I could not carry all the bottles. As well as saline solution and glucose there was Ringer lactate – that, too, had been administered to the girls at Nødebogård. He would have to carry them himself, maybe feeling he had to shoulder some of the responsibility would help to keep him awake.

I let us in to the little office next to Hessen's clinic. From there, through the Mensendieck mirror, we could watch Katarina and the director.

He had taken a seat and was facing us. He had white hair and sideburns like Grundtvig, but was smaller and slicker. His lips were moving, but you could not hear anything. Very carefully I set the door ajar.

"We've brought him up," said Katarina, "so that you can see him."

One of the tubes had slipped out of August's nose. There was no probe inside it, so it was probably meant for something else, oxygen maybe, they had usually prescribed that at Nødebogård. I used this tube to tie his hands behind his back, not tightly, mainly for show.

"That won't be necessary," said Baunsbak-Kold; "I've read the file."

I put on the white coat. This was my own idea, it was not part of the plan. Then I opened the door, pushed August in and positioned him in the middle of the room.

The Director of Education got to his feet and stepped back a bit. I need not have worried about him seeing the splatters of paint on the coat, he did not look at me at all.

"How do you do, young man?" he said to August. "My name is Baunsbak-Kold."

To this August made no reply. He seemed to be asleep on his feet.

"I've tied his hands together," I said, "there's no risk. And he's been given four Mogadon."

"I hear you're feeling better," he said.

August made no reply to this either.

161

"Take him away," he said.

He had not looked directly at August. He had not been able to bring himself to do it.

"He has attacked a teacher," said Katarina. "He will not eat. We have had him admitted on a red warrant. He broke two of Superintendent Flakkedam's fingers when we brought him up here. We have him under round-the-clock surveillance. We can no longer be held responsible, we need endorsement."

He had turned to face the window. From there you could look across the grounds to Copenhagen.

"It must be all over town by now," he said. "I suppose Hårdrup was informed long ago?"

Aage Hårdrup, theologian and educator, was the State Inspector assigned to the school. You had seen him at close quarters just once, when he made a speech at the inauguration of the annexe and the new toilets.

"You're the first to hear of it," said Katarina. "We feel the less that's said about it the better."

"Parliament sits less than three kilometres away as the crow flies," he said. "This is all going to rebound on me."

He stuck his hand into his pocket – for a handkerchief, I thought – but it was a comb. Unaware of what he was doing, he combed both his hair and his sideburns.

"This has gone too far," he said. "I told Biehl so months ago. This boy has to go back to Sandbjerggård. The worst of the others must be sent back where they came from, I'll attend to that person-ally. Although, of course, we cannot altogether put a stop to this. Too much is expected of it. At the highest level."

I had not so much listened to his words as sensed him. He had worked himself up, I knew that it was about to come to a head.

"What does Biehl have to say?" he said.

Katarina did not get the chance to reply. There was no transition. One moment he was speaking, the next he was yelling like a madman.

"What in hell's name does Biehl have to say!"

Never before at the school had an adult sworn or used abusive language, never, this had been a cast-iron rule.

"Sorry," he said. "I'm sorry . . ."

I led August from the room and pulled the door to behind us, but did not close it. Very gently I sat him on a chair, took off the tape and removed the drips. He started to pull the tube out of his throat by himself.

Baunsbak-Kold sat down opposite Katarina.

"It is, of course, my responsibility," he said.

He looked straight at the mirror, I knew he could not see us. He seemed very tired now.

"I've read his file," he said. "I just cannot conceive of it. Such brutality. Violence. And between children and parents."

"Have you never hit your children?" said Katarina.

At first he just clammed up, then he answered. Slowly, as though he were surprised by the question, and perhaps by his own reply.

"I've spanked them," he said. "Well, one does. But they've never hit back."

He closed his eyes. I knew he was picturing the photographs from the police report.

When next he spoke, his voice was weak as a child's.

"One has seen it in the newspapers. It has drawn closer. The unaccountable children. Now he is lying on my desk. How can such a thing happen? The brutality. Why does it happen? Isn't that your field? Isn't that what you're paid to do – to explain it?"

She did not answer him.

"It's beyond my powers," he said.

I remembered the clock. Since Katarina had given me the wrist-watch I had regularly remembered the time. As though I were becoming less ill. Now, when it was all too late, anyway.

I had seven minutes.

"There was no opposing Biehl," he said. "From the first meeting at the Ministry it was a *fait accompli*. Surely you noticed it too?"

"I was not there," said Katarina.

"No. True enough. Hessen was. 'Man is a divine experiment which proves how spirit and dust can merge.' Fascinating, isn't it? Grundtvig – in the preface to *Norse Mythology*. He had built his speech around it. We were only going to continue this experiment. Turn the school into 'the workshop of the sun' – that, too, is Grundtvig, from *New Year's Morning*. It sounds so plausible when he says it. 'We act in the hope of future glory.' You must have seen that, after all it turns up several times in his writing."

"Where?"

"In the applications."

"Where are they?" she asked.

He did not get her drift.

"They are arranged in the same way as the Ministry Circulars, by date. They cover November and December 1969. They're all there, in the office, on those shelves. I've referred to them myself several times."

For a moment he had been on the verge of coming unstuck. Now, gradually, he regained his composure.

"It was an idea that seemed born to succeed. He carries everyone with him. Me, the Minister, the Department, the Charity Schools Foundation, the Educational Institute, Hårdrup. The money is there. The wheels start to turn. It all bodes so well. And then these breakdowns start to occur. At least in the residential schools they were out of the way. But this is a reputable school, a model, on the outskirts of the capital. And now the grants have been awarded and partially spent. There's no stopping it now, the forces that have been set in motion are too great, too much is at stake."

I got up. Four minutes to go.

"If that were all there was to it," he said. "But then there are the children's interests to be considered. Like that one, that little chap. What burden is he carrying?"

He buried his face in his hands. I went over to the door.

"I must go," he said.

The corridor was deserted. The staff-room door was at the far end. I opened it and stepped inside.

Pupils had no business in the staff room. I had never been there.

It was big. There were sofas, and fabric on the chairs. In the classroom you sat on wooden chairs or at a desk. The teacher's chair had a leather seat, but nowhere else was there upholstered furniture.

It smelled of coffee and good food. Not packed lunches, nor like what came out of the kitchen in the annexe. Good food.

One of the kitchen staff, in her overall, was in the room, and two of the new teachers were sitting there, doing some marking. Fredhøj was standing by one of the windows.

"Excuse me," I said, "I was sent with a message for Hessen."

Then I closed the door.

There had been pictures on the wall, you noticed them right away. Sticking things up on the classroom walls was not permitted – to save wear and tear. There had also been a big electric clock. But nothing that could have been the school bell.

I ran along the corridor to the door next to Fredhøj's office – the one Katarina had spoken of – and unlocked it. Then I stepped inside and locked it behind me.

It was a very narrow room, but deep. On the wall to my left, behind glass, there was a small plate with a push button. The school fire alarm, it said. Next to it hung a notice giving the procedure for evacuation.

Other than that, the room held nothing but the clock.

It was fixed to the wall. So high up that it was beyond the reach of any living soul. The actual works were enclosed within a locked casing. There was a glass panel in the cover. You could see the face and a long pendulum. Under the face there was a gearwheel, of a sort you had never come across before. I had two minutes left.

I took off my shoes and socks, placed one foot on either wall, and ascended on high.

A year earlier, two girls from the class above us had turned up at school barefoot.

Naturally Biehl had spotted them right away in the playground, and yet he had let them pass. The first period had gone by without comment.

At Assembly they had been isolated. Fredhøj had positioned them next to the lectern. Then Biehl had come. He proceeded with Assembly in the normal way. Everyone had known that something was up, everyone knew the girls. They had written a song for the school play, and it had been banned. One of them was said to have had gonorrhoea the year before.

At the end of the patriotic song the hall had grown quiet. Biehl had waited until the awareness was absolutely concentrated. Then he had said that the school welcomed intelligent and accurate criticism of the established order, but the method which these so-called Provos had chosen was both futile and stupid. As far as long hair and bare feet were concerned, everyone was entitled to their own opinion. What was, however, beyond a shadow of a doubt was that such unhygienic and downright disgusting habits would not be countenanced in this school. He would now ask the two girls standing beside him to go home and give this some careful thought. And they need not come back until they felt that they had understood.

I remembered this now. It meant that I had to force myself to set foot on the walls. Never before had you so much as brushed against them. Yet here you were, and with bare feet into the bargain.

"Bürk", it said, on the clock. I wedged myself tight and opened the cover.

It was lifeless. It moved, but it was not alive – that is what I told myself. But still I could not cope with touching it.

Electrical cables ran into the casing, but not to the works. The works were hand-wound. Two keys lay on the floor of the casing, and there was a pawl in the face. Above the pawl sat a small dial that shifted once every second. One minute to go.

There were labels stuck to the back of the casing, with warnings printed in German. I could read these only with some difficulty. But I could tell, from the exclamation marks and the underlining, that these were the directions for winding the clock. In addition to the keys, on the floor of the casing, there was a box of 2.5 A fuses and a slip of paper with details of when the works had been adjusted. An adjustment of about one minute had been made at the end of each month.

I tried pushing the big hand backwards. Impossible. It seemed to be stuck fast, there was nothing to be done about it.

The gearwheel below the works was connected to a fair amount of machinery, it was impossible to figure it all out in such a short time. What was clear, however, was that it had to be connected to the bell mechanism, which was electric. Inside the casing there was a relay marked "Tradania, Denmark". The works themselves were German, so the clock was, in fact, the result of German-Danish co-operation.

The gearwheel was divided up from one to twenty-four, with twelve small perforations for every hour. In the perforations corresponding to when the bell rang sat a very tiny screw. The clock had, therefore, a built-in accuracy of better than plus/minus a couple of minutes.

Also on the casing floor was a little screwdriver. I used this to remove the screws that would have closed the circuit, here, ten seconds later.

Then the door was unlocked and in came Fredhøj. He looked down the room. Then he went over to the window and looked out. Then he walked back to the door.

He did not look up, he did not see me.

It was not luck. It was because he would never have dreamed of it, because the thought never occurred to him.

He could not. Well, he had never looked upwards for children. They had always been beneath him. Down in the class, or down in the playground, or down in the hall, or down in the church, always down. He could no longer lift his face towards the ceiling and the light. Not to catch sight of a child.

I saw him from above. As I had never before seen a teacher. I saw his dandruff. On his scalp and on his jacket.

He went out and locked the door behind him.

I moved the screws. For the rest of the day there were ten more. Ten minutes had now disappeared from the school day and from the universe, as though they had never been. Staying up there was not easy, but I forced myself. There was no strength left, though, for climbing down once it was done. I fell the last part of the way and could not get up right away. Then Oscar Humlum sat down beside me.

I had not seen him, but he must have been there all the time.

"We're going home soon," I said.

He made me aware of my foot. It had swollen up straight away. There was no way of getting it into the shoe, but I got the sock on.

I told him that I had better see about getting home now, with August and Katarina, and wouldn't he like to come too, how about it?

He shook his head. Maybe it was that apprenticeship on the Swedish ferries, maybe it was something else. He started to leave.

I called after him, he stopped and turned.

"There's something you should know," I said. "Since we met, ever since that first time when we each sat on a toilet, up against the radiator, ever since then I have never been completely alone, even after you left me. Before that there had never really been anything in my life. But once someone has stood under the cold shower just so that you can stay in the warm one, then you can never really be totally alone again."

I let myself out into the corridor and was sure that disaster had struck.

The door of the office was flung open and the secretary came running out. I knew that now I would have to take her into the clock room and get her to keep absolutely quiet for a while, however that was to be done. That was as far as I got in my thinking.

She did not look at me at all. She cut across the corridor and ran out on to the south stairway, you could hear her clattering down it.

Katarina came walking out of the office at her back.

We stood there, face to face, in the corridor – the worst of all possible places – caught in a little eddy in the stream of time.

"I told her a car had been smashed," she said, "one that looked like hers. I said a Taunus had reversed into it, that I had recognised the Director of Education, then he had driven off. I said the Mascot looked like a concertina, and didn't she want to go down and check."

She had a big cardboard folder under her arm. There were some dates marked on the outside. The way she was holding the folder I could not see them, but I knew it would have to do with November and December 1969.

"Once you start lying," she said, "it just gets easier and easier."

August had woken up a bit. When we came in, he put his finger to his lips. The loudspeaker.

Very softly I went in to it. It was giving off sounds, a crackling that rose and fell, there was no way of telling whether they were looking for us, or what was the matter – only that something was going on.

168

When I came back, Katarina was standing looking at the filing cabinet.

"Can it be opened?" she said.

My first reaction was to say no, but I opened it anyway.

She found our files. Then she counted the others.

"Sixty," she said. "They're testing sixty pupils. What for?"

August said, "I'm cold."

We shared out what clothes we had. Katarina gave him boots and tights, which left her in a dress and with bare legs. She got my shoes which I could not use anyway because of my foot, which had got bigger. August put on his vest and I gave him my sweater.

Plaintive voices were now rising to us from the depths. Katarina went over to the window. "Klastersen has had our class in the main hall," she said.

The main hall was used for ball games. A different time applied there. To get the full physical benefit of the PE classes the intervals on either side were suspended, to allow for showers and changing. So there was no bell in the main hall. Klastersen controlled the periods with a stopwatch. The showers and changing rooms were in the main building, which was locked during lessons, to prevent strangers from the outside getting in and committing acts of vandalism or theft. What had happened now was that Klastersen had sent the pupils over to shower and they had found the main building locked, because the bell had not rung as it should, and so the teacher on playground duty had not unlocked the door. Now they were hanging about in the snow, in shorts and gym shoes.

Then Biehl spoke over the loudspeaker.

"Andersen," he said, "report to the office."

It was the first time ever that anyone had been summoned over the loudspeaker.

"He's off duty," said Katarina, "Andersen's off duty."

She did not have her timetable with her, but still she knew, she must have had it off by heart.

"They want him to open the door to the bell," I said.

"Why don't they do it themselves?"

"They can't," I said. "I snapped off the key, the end of the key's stuck in the lock."

At that moment, the bell rang.

Just as it sounded, there was a pause. Then silence. It was almost absolute.

It should not have been there, there should have been voices and people in the corridor, but instead the school now seemed dead. I could tell from the others' faces that they did not understand it.

"It's the teachers," I said, "they're confused. The bell's ten minutes late in going off. They don't know whether it's rung for a class or an interval, and no one's had their break. Right now they don't know what they're supposed to do. It will only take a moment, then people will come out into the corridors."

"There's something else, too," said August.

He had got to his feet, the sweater came down to his knees.

"They don't dare let people downstairs. They know the kind of racket there is in the playground. During periods it's like you're dead, but the playground's jumping. Haven't you noticed the way the teacher on playground duty keeps to the edge? It only works at all because they have the bell. It's like a knife, the only thing that can cut through. Without it they would never get people back up. Now they don't know whether it's working. They don't dare send people down."

He was not steady on his feet, especially not in Katarina's boots. But I had noticed before that once he got started – on drawing or something – he did not stop until he ran up against something solid.

"Right now they're sitting at their desks, not letting on. But everyone knows there's something wrong, the pressure in the classroom is rising and rising. Then you get an idea. You remember that there's only one teacher, but there are twenty of you, no one stands a chance against twenty, not even with the infants, if they set their minds to it. So you look round about and then your imagination lends a hand. Everyone has a pencil sharpener – it's compulsory, isn't it – so you work the blade free, it may be small, but it's like a razor blade, then you get up and walk over to the teacher's desk, and it's over, a moment more and he's lying there and then you pelt out into freedom . . ."

170

"Oh yeah," said Katarina, "with straps on your arms and legs, two drips and a rubber tube up your nose."

He had been a long way off, but he came down like a shot and was at her side in a single movement.

"So what was that about your father and mother, chummie?" he said.

I had managed to get between them. His eyes were fixed on me. He, who rarely looked at anyone.

Under his skin another person had taken over, danger threatened.

Even so, I could not hit – I could not hit a child, come what may.

I stuck my left hand out towards him, with the fingers that were taped together. I did not try to protect myself.

"Why don't you just break them in another place?" I said.

He checked himself and then seized up. He did not look at the hand.

"It wasn't me," he said. "What're we waiting for, what happens next?"

At that moment Biehl's voice came over the loudspeaker once again.

"The time is now 13.00," he said. "All classes will go to the play-ground immediately. There will be an interval until 13.20."

Katarina stood there, listening, leaning towards the sound.

"He's scared," she said.

She had spoken right beside the loudspeaker; I put a hand over her mouth.

The voice came again, very clear, as though he were right beside us.

"Will all teachers, apart from those on playground duty, please report to the staff room immediately."

Katarina removed my hand.

"It was something you said," she said. " 'Time is something you have to hold on to'. It's the pauses they're scared of."

We were still standing right beside the loudspeakers, we should not have spoken.

"He's not scared," I said. "He's the one who talked about the eloquent pauses."

171

"We're not talking about them. This is different. These pauses are out of control. Time and planning are falling apart."

Then Biehl's voice came again, but he did not get the chance to finish.

"To all classes. Anyone having seen, or seeing, Peter from Primary VII, August Joon . . ."

He got no further. August struck just once, but the blow went through the fabric and crushed the grill behind. Then he grabbed the casing and butted it – shattering the membrane and pulling the loudspeaker loose. Then I got to him and led him away. He was bleeding, the loudspeaker dangled by its cables, we had been cut off.

Now we could hear the building. Distant voices, stairs vibrating. We stood absolutely still, listening to this. We looked at Katarina.

Up until this point it had been her plan. This was as far as we had got in the storehouse.

"Now what?" said August.

Of course, in a way, we had been depending on her.

She did not answer him. She just stood there, straight-backed, looking at us. And then I realised that she had no answer.

"I know what you thought," said August. "You thought something would probably turn up."

I had a grip on him, but he was calm. It was as though he had given up.

"You thought, well . . . there's always the family. I bet you have an uncle in some ministry or other who can just get on to Biehl and have a word with him, am I right? And after this school there'll be another, the one your cousins go to – Busse's or Classen's. But, d'you wanna know something? For us, for me, and for Daft Peter, for us there's . . ."

At first he could not get it out. It filled his body and made it seize up, made it hard as stone. Then it relaxed, and he said it.

"For us there's nothing," he said. "Nothing but a black hole."

Her expression did not change. Her eyes seemed to darken, become almost black. Then the tears began to flow. No change in her face, just tears streaming from the dark hollows of her eyes.

The time had come for me to take charge, to protect them.

"We're going home," I said.

We got ready to leave. She was gathering up the papers. She noticed at once.

"Where's August's file?" she said.

"I've put it back," I said.

It was impossible to explain it to her. For her it was so important to know. You would never be able to make her understand that sometimes it may be more of a help not to know.

She said nothing. Maybe she had understood after all.

We listened at the door until the last of the teachers had let themselves into the corridor, then we descended by the south stairs. We met no one. The playground, too, was deserted. There was a risk that we would be spotted from Andersen's house. But luck was on our side. We got all the way along the main building and the main hall and out into the grounds without being challenged.

It had been snowing, and now the fog had come down. We walked into the fog and were gone.

$$\overset{\textstyle 14}{\bigcirc}$$

AUGUST KEPT FALLING DOWN. We held on to him, one on either side. My socks were no use against the snow, but when I stopped feeling my feet I did not feel the bad foot – the one that had got bigger – either.

We could see nothing but the whiteness. I lost my bearings a couple of times, and then Humlum showed himself – just a glimpse – to let us know we were on the right track.

From the very beginning it had been written that it would be thus. There would be a journey through the wilderness, but it would be easier to bear because those you hold dear, the woman and the child, are by your side. At last you would reach the promised land.

Out of the fog it rose. The sign said "Storehouse", but we saw now that this had always been to keep people away. We had always been intended to find our way to this place.

Everything was as Katarina and I had left it.

I bolted the door and arranged boxes round the table, to make it cosy. The cold was a problem. I thought of lighting a fire, but there was no flue and they would have been able to see the light, and there were cans of petrol for the lawnmowers all over the place. But, in one of the cabinets, I found some old copies of *World of Nature*. We stuffed these into August's vest and down into his tights. He had got worse, but that would soon pass now we were able to care for him.

We sat round the table. They were both tired and kept nodding off. Soon they were asleep.

*   *   *

I kept watch over them. I had brought them here, they were my responsibility now. August was propped up in the corner, Katarina had rested her head on the table. I could hear their breathing – August's was rapid, hers was slower. I watched over them – the woman and the child – that no evil should befall them.

Then I saw Oscar Humlum, sort of in the background.

"Go to sleep," he said. "I'll keep watch."

So I dozed for a bit, but something woke me. Oscar was sitting looking at me.

"It's the hunger," he said, "that's why you can't sleep. It comes in waves. When it comes, you have to feel it. Don't think about anything else, or about food, but look upon it with the light of awareness."

I tried and the hunger came and then departed from me.

"Where did you learn that?" I said. "You didn't know about it back then."

"I'm bigger now though," he said; "that's the chance that comes with the passage of time and growing up. The pain doesn't get any easier. But you become better at dealing with it."

I could see now that he did look older, and more peaceful.

"You can stay here, with us," I said, "always. No one's ever going to expel anyone again."

He did not answer, he just motioned to me to go to sleep.

When I awoke August had come round. He was sitting reading the applications and the files. Katarina had left them on the table. He was restless.

He wanted me to take the papers, I refused; he held them out to Katarina.

"I read them while you were sleeping," she said.

He started to read aloud.

" 'To the Department of Primary and Lower-Secondary Education. Biehl's Academy hereby requests the permission of the Department to proceed with the project, for which provisional plans were submitted to the Department at the meeting on 11 November 1969, and of which fuller details are appended.' "

He lowered the paper.

"This is the proof," he said.

He leafed through the pile, picking out papers at random. When he read, it was slowly and with difficulty, his voice seemed to be fumbling around among the words.

" 'As rector of Biehl's Academy I take the liberty of applying both for the Ministry of Education's approval of the experimental project more fully detailed in the enclosed letter, and for a grant from the Ministry's appropriations fund for experimental studies, to cover the costs of implementing the project.'

"It's a conspiracy," he said. "They've got it all worked out. They've rounded people up. Now they're to be destroyed."

"Integrated," said Katarina. "They want to take children from the treatment homes and reformatories and put them back into ordinary schools. Integration. That's the plan."

Oscar signalled to me, then I heard it. Andersen's Rottweiler. But he gave me a reassuring wave.

August's voice went on and on, he was lost in the papers now, " '. . . following consultation with educational and psychological experts, additional application is hereby made for the defraying, by the Charity Schools Foundation, of those costs incurred in the appointment of a superintendent for Biehl's boarding school, in as much as . . .' "

He stopped.

"That's Flakkedam," he said. "The experiment is supposed to start here. And then it's to spread. Why is it secret? It says here it has to be kept secret. What is this?"

They were the same transcripts as had been in his folder in Biehl's office.

"It's from the court records," I said. "They must have had the sanction of the Ministry of Justice, those are confidential."

"He writes that it's for the children's sake," she said. "So that they can go on being children for as long as possible. And not be encumbered with adult responsibilities. That's what he's always believed."

"Yes," I said. "He said the same thing when he refused to set up a student council."

August was so restless now that he could no longer sit still. He had got up, he put his hands on the cupboards and kind of felt his way along them. Oscar was no longer looking at me but at Katarina.

"He writes that the experiment is ahead of its time," she said.

176

"That it belongs to the future. That it is ahead of public opinion. Therefore it would be better to carry it out discreetly. And not unveil it until you could produce some convincing results."

August had disappeared towards the back of the room, out of sight. But you could hear him pacing around in the darkness.

"But it all went wrong for them," she said. "They must have thought they could help, turn the school into 'the workshop of the sun' like he said. Into a laboratory where the differences between those who were damaged and those who were normal would be eliminated. That's why you two were accepted. And it explains Hessen and all those tests. That's why they appointed Flakkedam. To take care of security."

I could see his eyes now. In the darkness they gathered the last of the light, like those of a wild animal.

"But what about Karin Ærø's stars?" I said. "And the beatings. And the marks and the schedules. There's still no explanation for them."

"No," she said. "Behind their plan there has to be another one. One they know nothing about."

"So who knows about it, then?" said August.

"Something greater than them."

Suddenly he was right in front of her, I would have done something, but I did not have a chance. It had even taken Humlum by surprise, he had not got to his feet either.

"There's nothing above them," said August. "They've got it all worked out. That's why they've got to go, one way or another . . ."

That was his strategy. To hate. But then it had to be directed at someone, it could not just be there. And those you hated had to be the ones who were responsible. Well, I mean otherwise they, personally, would not be guilty.

"It's no good," she said. "There's something greater behind them."

She was very aware. Not just of him, but of something else, something that surrounded us. She was close to something crucial.

"There's nothing behind them but a black hole!"

He had screamed. He turned away, pushed in a pane of glass in the cabinet with the flat of his hand, pressed his palm against the ring of glass that was left and started to run it round. Only then did Humlum get to him, and pull him back, then I took over.

Katarina stood there, ramrod-straight, she had not moved. I kept hold of him with one hand, while with the other I took off my shirt, ripped off a sleeve and bound it round his hand. Then he got away from me.

He walked along the cabinets looking through the glass at the things on the shelves, the stuffed animals. He had to lean against them to stay on his feet.

"It's like at home," he said. "Twelve of everything from the good old days. They're locked up too – no sticky fingers on them. I could do with a fag."

I handed him a pack, they were his own – and the matches. I had tucked them away before they came for his things, after he was admitted to the sickbay.

He lit it himself, but then it slipped through his fingers, he bent down and picked it up. He inhaled and broke into a bout of coughing.

"Christ, that's good," he said.

He had the cigarette caught in at the bandage. It was already very wet. Once everything had been settled I would clean the wound and put on a proper bandage.

"She has to take the bus now," he said. "Mum, I mean, even though she hates it. To stand and hold on to bars that people have touched, even with net gloves. When I get back, I'll buy her a car."

He seemed to be talking in his sleep. Katarina led him back to the table and got him to sit down. There was a coating of sweat on his forehead. She supported his head with one hand and, with the palm of the other, she wiped away the sweat.

"Nobody touches me," he said.

But he let her do it.

We sat around the table. August had slumped towards Katarina. She did not touch him. But she moved closer, so he could sit comfortably.

Outside, in the darkness, there was some activity. I looked over at Oscar Humlum, he shook his head. "Not yet," he said.

August and Katarina were sitting looking at me, it was all okay. They did not assess me. Nor did they want me to achieve anything

178

further. I had brought them here and everything was as it should be.

I saw how pure, in a way, they were – no matter what they had done. Each in their own way they had tried to stay what they were. Not like me, who had never been anything, and so had been trying all my life to be someone else. To come inside.

I saw that they understood this, too. That they understood it and that it was okay. That, even so, I mattered, come what may.

And then time, too, faded away. I saw how small August was, like the child I would later have, even though he was older. In that moment, those two became as one, he and the child, and thus it became impossible ever again to separate them completely.

I stretched a hand across the table and stroked his hair. He let me do it. Beneath my hand it grew warm and quite smooth. Soon he was sleeping. Katarina was watching me.

I looked around.

"Humlum," I said.

She nodded, as if she had known all along.

" 'Save yourself' ," I said, "that was the last thing he said. He knew we couldn't both get away. It would have been like too much contamination for the school to export at one time. He stood there with the rope in his hands. Then he cocked his head and listened for the train. His sight wasn't so good. In the winter, in the toilets, he had told me that when he was nine years old he had been with a foster family who lived on Genforeningspladsen. They used to wake him at half-past three in the morning and send him across to N. L. Dehn's Institutional Laundry where everybody pretended he was fourteen, because then it wouldn't be child labour, and there he wheeled the clothes from the dry-cleaning machine to the woman who did the ironing. The man on the dry-cleaning machine used to turn up drunk for work and one day there was something to do with a tap and Humlum got sprayed in the eyes with cleaning fluid, and then he'd been taken away from that family. But from then on he didn't see too well at all. Instead he located the train by its sound, this time too.

" 'I'll stay here,' " I said; " 'if you don't do it, I'll stay.'

"He smiled, he did not hear me, already he was in another world.

"He pushed off, pretty much in the normal way, with the right timing. But when it came to the end of the swing he just hung there.

He stretched out this last moment of his life so long that the return swing was delayed, but at last he began to move, like a pendulum, and then came the train."

Katarina did not say a word, she just nodded.

I did not look up at Oscar, it was not necessary, we both knew it had been the right thing to do, laying it out for her.

August said something. Because of the fever it sounded as though it came to us from a distant room.

"Maybe a person can be born to the wrong people," he said. "Maybe a person should have been put somewhere else."

He said it, but we had all thought it, all four of us, Oscar too.

"Do you get another crack at it?" he asked.

He asked in such a peaceful way. The way a child asks its mother, but more as an equal. And that is how she answered him.

"Back then," she said, "with my Mum and Dad, I didn't believe it would ever stop hurting. That happiness would ever come again. But it's better now, and now and again, despite everything, it is there. So in a way you do."

"But what about something you've done to someone?"

She did not answer that. Somewhere in the darkness the dog barked.

"I'm scared of dogs," he said.

I would have liked to read to them.

They had not read to us at Crusty House, nor at Himmelbjerg House – it was considered soppy. But at the Christian Foundation they did.

Once you had experienced it, it was impossible to forget. In the mornings it had been the Thought for the Day, from the bottom corner of the *Christian Daily*; in the evenings, the Bible. Even so, you had looked forward to it. The matron, Sister Ragna, did the reading. She read standing up, from the end of the dormitory. It had made it easier to fall asleep. Entering the night was always the hardest part. It is easier to keep things at bay when it is light. When it grows dark, they come pouring in.

I wanted to read to them. This was the most difficult time of day for August. And there was no medicine to give him. I wanted to ease his way into the darkness.

There was *World of Nature*, but that seemed out of the question. And the only thing that came to mind was the Bible. That was no good, it was too close to the sisters and to Biehl.

So I chose to say whatever came into my head.

"We take a boat," I said, "big enough to live on. We sail southwards, where it's warmer. On a boat you can never be expelled, you always have the right to stay where you are, and you're always together. In the evenings we can sit and listen to the water. When I'm twenty-one we'll adopt you."

Maybe he wasn't awake. Maybe he was sleeping, which had been the idea. But Katarina was listening to me.

As a rule, what you imagine is not like real life. As a rule it is worse. This moment was just exactly as I had pictured it. I had pictured how a family would sit together. Just like this.

"I'm sorry if I've hurt you two," she said.

She was just to forget it, I said. Everything had turned out fine. But what about her mother and father, I said. And what about the experiment?

"I suppose I thought I could get to meet them again," she said. "But it doesn't work that way. That was just wishful thinking. But the experiment is coming to an end, anyway. At least, the first phase."

I did not want to get too close, by asking what she meant. But even though the question went unasked, she understood it. The way things were between us now, it was not necessary to say all that much.

"Time is no law of nature," she said. "It is a plan. When you look at it with awareness, or start to touch it, then it starts to disintegrate. That is the conclusion of the first phase of the experiment. This plan is not Biehl's. It's too big, too complete for that. The second phase will be to investigate what lies behind time. We have seen it start to fall apart. The next thing is to understand what lies behind it."

You could see by looking at her. She had to have an answer. It was a need about which she, personally, could do nothing. There was something I wanted to say to her, but it was impossible.

August was shaking badly. She took off her sweater and put it round him.

"If you come over here, it'll be easier for us to keep warm," she said.

She put her arm round August and I leaned against her. And then I said it anyway, the words just came out, there was nothing to be done about it. I told her I loved her. It was the first time I had ever got my tongue round the words.

I saw that they also applied to August. That you could not say something like that to the woman without it applying to the child as well.

She did not reply. Nor was it necessary. I had given, without needing something in return.

All three of us must have slept. When he spoke it still seemed to be in his sleep.

"If there is a second time," he said, "then they ought to suffer more. It was over too soon."

All the time we had known that he was lost.

15

IT WAS KATARINA who discovered it. She laid a hand on my arm.

"He's gone," she said.

It was light outside, due to the fog having lifted, and to the stars and the snow. We followed his tracks. He had been bleeding as he went, at one spot we found the bandage.

All the lights in the school were out, the building was in darkness, the windows were black. Just as it had looked to me, those nights when I had not slept. He had crossed the south playground, keeping close to the wall. He had got in by smashing a pane in the door. I had always thought it was careless to have a latch fixed next to a pane of glass.

We ascended to the fifth floor. He had left the door open and the light burning in the clinic, but had drawn the curtains. They were blackout curtains. Certain of the tests – Raven's progressive matrices for instance – involved slides.

To begin with, there was silence. Then you heard them in the corridor.

First you smelled Biehl's cigar. Then there was a brief pause, and then Biehl himself came in. He was looking for something, his head was right down at floor level. You had never supposed that he could bow so deeply, you had only ever seen him upright. He was in his dressing gown, and had his right arm up his back. The last part of him to come through the door was his hand. Behind him came August. He had hold of three of Biehl's fingers, all of them broken.

Behind August came Biehl's wife, Astrid, in her nightgown. She had always looked like a Norse goddess – willowy, ash-blonde and stately, even now.

The fever lay like a membrane over August's eyes. You could see how terrified he was. Like a little child. And yet quite determined. He, too, had now turned upon the pain. In order to erase it.

"I'm glad you came," he said.

He said it without recognising us. We were standing three metres away from him. He could no longer see as far as us.

He let Biehl lift his head a fraction.

"My Mum and Dad are here," he said. "To collect me."

Biehl had not looked at us. His awareness was on August.

"You know perfectly well what has happened to your mother and father," he said.

No visible movement, just the spongy crack as one of his fingers snapped in a fresh place. He fell to his knees.

You could not tell by looking at August.

His left hand was sort of hidden. I shifted position slightly, to get a look at it, the movement must have caught his eye because he brought it into the open. In it was Biehl's cigar, which was lit. That, and a two-litre bottle of petrol – he must have picked it up in the storehouse. In the bottle was a cork, between the cork and the glass he had crammed a strip off his bandage.

"It's like a wick," he said. "If I put the cigar to it and smash the bottle we all go sky-high."

Astrid Biehl was looking at my bare feet, I'd taken off my socks.

"I hurt myself," I said, "I couldn't get my foot into my shoe. It won't happen again."

They said nothing. Maybe because it was obvious from the bruising that I was telling the truth, maybe because they could not speak.

"We're just leaving," August said to Biehl. "We're going home. But before we go, you have to confess."

No one said a word.

He went on: "I could have stayed at home. We were fine, we could have sat together in the evenings, like we'd just been doing. Not too close together, nobody bothering anybody else, no need to be all over one another. But you're together, quiet and peaceful. If anyone feels like drawing they can just get some paper and a pencil, nothing will be said about it. No one goes on about your report card. No one gets hit. But then you're dragged up here. You're tied down at night, during the day Flakkedam sits behind you. Tell Mum how a thing like that can happen."

Biehl was on his knees, so his face was level with August's.

"We wanted to do good," he said.

Another finger broken.

All of a sudden Biehl's lips were like sandpaper. Grey and as though dusted with dried granules. He looked August in the eye.

"We wanted to help," he said. "Not just the children of the light. We wanted to carry the rest of you along with us. From the halls of the dead to the land of the living. We wanted to bring all of you together in the Danish Free School. Even those who suffer hardships but have a right to the light."

August's body was now shaking badly, even his face was out of control, it looked as though he were constantly making faces. Only the hand encircling Biehl's fingers did not move. It held the last of the life within him.

"What about the darkness inside people?" said Katarina.

"The light will disperse it," said Biehl.

August brought his face right down to Biehl's ear. They looked like two people exchanging confidences.

"There's not that much light in the whole world," he whispered.

He looked at Katarina. She was standing less than a metre from him, but it was obvious that his eyes were failing him. He stretched out a hand and felt her. With his left hand, the one holding the bottle and the cigar. He felt with the outer edge of the hand, up over her throat and cheek. The cigar end, the smoke and the bottle hung in the air before her eyes. She did not move.

"It'll be over soon," he said. "Then I'll come back to you. And we can sit the way we did back there. With Peter, too. Is he with you now?"

"Yes," she said.

"Can I keep the paper and pencils?"

"Yes," she said.

He stroked her cheek.

"Will you wait here for me?" he said.

She could not answer him.

"No more taking the bus," he said. "I've bought you a car. It's waiting down below."

He led Biehl over to the door.

"August!" she said.

He stopped.

"They have children," she said. "He's somebody's father."

To this he made no reply. He simply led Biehl out through the door, and then they were gone.

With that, Astrid Biehl turned and went out into the corridor. A door was unlocked. We heard her going into the room next door, the one with the school clock. They must have had the lock fixed. Every sound could be heard quite plainly – her bare feet on the floor, the soft crunch as she smashed the glass. Then the alarm went off.

It was the same signal as usual, sent over all the loudspeakers. But this time it kept going on and off, on and off, the noise was unbearable. We went out into the corridor and turned away from it, into the staff room.

It was dark, the only light was coming from outside – from the grounds and the sky and, further off, from Copenhagen. We stood by the window.

They came pretty quickly. Astrid Biehl must have met them in the driveway, once the searchlights had been lit you saw her several times, still in her nightgown.

They parked in a semicircle and left the car headlights on, in addition to switching on the searchlights. The storehouse sat there, like a black bull's-eye in the white snow. For a while, nothing happened. Then more cars arrived, you saw Fredhøj too, down there in the snow. Then peace and quiet descended. Very bright light, but otherwise nothing. Pause.

Then Biehl appeared. He came out of the shed, alone, but still bent double. His dressing gown had slipped half off him, he was partly naked. And in that state, he ran towards the searchlights.

Then came the fire. Not an explosion, not really. Not anything as violent as that. Just a very speedy combustion. First the flash from August's bottle then the blast, as the petrol cans for the lawnmowers caught fire. It blew out the windows and doors first, then it forced off the roof, letting in oxygen. It was all over in seconds.

Of course, where we were, so high up, we could not feel the heat, nor could we hear very much.

It did not help though. Even though we held each other tight and had our eyes closed, it did not help. The light pierced the eyelids – only for the briefest of moments, but still it seared into the brain. It hurt the body too. As if, even from way down there, the fire had reached up and peeled away the top layer of skin, leaving us like two burn marks, two scorched foetuses supporting one another.

I did not want to look. When, despite myself, I did look, it was at Katarina's face. It was turned towards the window, screwed up like the face of an incubator baby. The pain of an abandoned, newborn baby on a far-too-old face.

And yet even then – I remember it now – deep down, but distinct: awareness. The need to understand.

FIRST THEY TRANSFERRED ME to Lars Olsen's Memorial
Home, Engbækgård, 2990 Nivå. There I prepared the first draft of
my report.

Lars Olsen's Memorial Home had the country's first secure unit for
children under fifteen years of age – walled in, no door handles on
the inside, a small, barred window set high up, table and bench
screwed to the floor, and you had to ring for the duty officer when
you needed the toilet.

Before you could be put there they had to have the special permission of the department and the longest they could keep you
there was two months, that was the law. However, dispensation
was given in my case, since there was the death of a schoolfellow
to be taken into account. I spent six months and eleven days there,
in strict isolation. This, inevitably, did me damage.

In those days they were not so shy of using solitary confinement.
It was considered to have a powerfully educative effect, like waiting
outside Biehl's office. The department's representative said that now
I would have plenty of time for reflection.

At Himmelbjerg House and at the Royal Orphanage you had
often been isolated and locked up in various places – mostly the
cellars, but other places too. At the Orphanage the standard punishment for being late three times in a row was royal guard duty – in
an empty broom cupboard under a picture of King Frederik and
Queen Ingrid. You stood from eight in the morning until six in
the evening, but even though it was in the dark and standing to

attention, it was, of course, nothing compared to six months and eleven days.

Even so you could have coped with it, others before you had coped. But when they transferred me I must have been weakened by what had happened, and by the fact that I had got used to talking to Katarina and August.

If those who listen, those who are your friends, are, nevertheless, to be taken from you, then it would have been better if you had never got to know them.

Since then there has been something about closed doors, or being in a room with several other people. Many years later – after my adoption and when I had completed my education and been to university – I tried working. I taught at the Institute of Physical Education at Odense University. I was there for a year and a half, then it became overwhelming. It kept coming and going – the fear of being alone like back then. Just when you were faced with twenty people, and all the responsibility, then came the feeling that they were going to leave you and lock the door behind them and there would not even be a button so you could ring for the duty officer. Furthermore, I worried about being late, so I used to get there hours ahead of time. But still the fear was there. After a year and a half I had to give it up.

If I had not been shown the way into the laboratory it would have been difficult, if not impossible, to hold one's own in society, to find a place in the outside world.

Here, too, the door is closed. But the child and I have come to an agreement. We both find closed doors difficult. According to the agreement, if it gets too difficult, then it is permitted to knock on the door and say so. And then the other one has to open the door to the one who is not feeling so good.

I was there for an indefinite period. Nevertheless, I found a way out – through the books. I found the books and with their help I drew up the report, in the form of a speech. I knew there would be a confrontation.

That was the way the department did things, by confrontation. When violence or abuse had been ascertained to have occurred in an institution, or if any other acts of negligence were suspected, where it was the adults' word against the children's, then a confrontation was arranged, this was a rule.

All doubt could thus be eliminated. In this way it would be possible to discover the absolute and definitive truth as to what had occurred. Then the blame could be apportioned and the guilty party be punished.

With this in mind I prepared the speech. I expected it to be addressed to Biehl and Fredhøj and Karin Ærø, and to the Department's representatives, and to Katarina.

In a way I also expected August to be there. Even though that was an insane thought.

As an excuse, I just want to point out how things were while the work was in progress. I could no longer tell day from night.

Now, later on, it can be seen that we had in fact understood most of it.

They had had a grand plan. Of bringing all children together under the Danish state-school system, including the mentally defective and delinquent, including the slow pupils – everyone right down to the borderliners with severe retardation. Biehl's Academy was to be turned into the model for this integration. The school was to have been a laboratory, a workshop for the study of how the integration should be brought about. Whatever this would require in the way of security arrangements, psychological assistance and extra tuition.

The orderliness and precision of the school were to form the firm, secure structure around this experiment.

Over the past couple of years I have gradually unearthed most of the papers from that time. Some of them are kept at the Department for Primary and Lower-Secondary Education, some at the Educational Institute and at Queen Amalie's Charity Schools Foundation, and at the Teacher Training College on Emdrupvej.

According to these, fifty-four major experiments on the integration of disadvantaged pupils into Danish state schools were run between 1964 and 1974. Fifty-four.

But even today, looking back on it, the experiment at Biehl's was something out of the ordinary.

When I read the applications they made back then, for money and support for the project, I do not understand them.

They are like Biehl's memoirs. So eloquent. So well-intentioned. But still somehow totally unrelated to what really happened. As though they have had a wonderful, visionary theory about time and children and fellowship.

And then – strictly isolated from this theory – there have been the actions they carried out.

Gaining access to the archives has been so surprisingly easy. I have been met with outright helpfulness. Back when it happened, they did everything they could to keep it hidden. At that time suppression, discretion, was one of the school's fundamental principles. Now the protection of any information whatsoever no longer seems to be important.

Maybe most people are of the same mind as Oscar and August, when they come to me in the laboratory and say I should abandon the work, because the '70s were so long ago, it is over and done with, it is too late.

Often I have had that thought: over and done with and too late.

When such thoughts present themselves, I know that I am thinking like an adult. Growing up means first of all to forget, and thereafter disown what was important when you were a child. To this I have then raised objections.

Even if it was over and too late, and altogether pretty insignificant, still it was your life. And around that, everything since then has revolved.

But it was not insignificant. Of that I have since become certain.

Their plan was directed at the entire universe, of that I have become certain. And such a plan cannot be disregarded.

In the applications they talk only about helping the delinquents and the mildly retarded and mildly defective – those were the words, in the undertakings for the grants. But in their minds or at the back of their minds, like a distant goal, they had the whole world. "We work for future glory," wrote Biehl. They felt that time was on their side, that they were working with something that would spread and inspire first the entire state-school system and then the rest of the country. If it had to be put into words they only mentioned groups of children. But their goal was the universe.

Biehl, Fredhøj, Karin Ærø, Baunsbak-Kold, State Inspector Aage Hårdrup, Hessen, Flakkedam, the department representatives. All of them were certain that they were defending eternal values. They have not said it straight out, they may not have thought it straight out either. But somewhere inside themselves and among themselves they have been completely and utterly certain that they were right, and that, with future generations of children who grew up, their ideas and thoughts could fly out into the world and spread across the country and beyond, maybe as far as the Moors. That it would be possible, sometime in the not too distant future, to have everyone respect their ideal of diligence and precision. And on that day, all living things in the universe would live at peace with one another.

I know this was their goal. It is not what you could call run-of-the-mill. You would have to call it colossal.

This goal was the subject of my report.

It went against common practice in the Home and was also at variance with the corrective effect of isolation to give me pencil and paper. What I found out, I therefore had to commit to memory.

*   *   *

I was, however, given books. I based my speech upon what I read in them. It was carefully planned, with an introduction, a discourse and a conclusion. When the day dawned I went in and presented it, in a clear, distinct voice. That was the last word. After that, there was nothing more to be said.

This is not true. I see that I have written it. But it is a lie. When the confrontation came, I said nothing of what had been in my mind, not a word.

There was no speech. By the time I had been at Lars Olsen's Memorial Home for a few weeks there was no memory left in which to store it. By then there was nothing but chaos.

I had a relapse, too, and hit a male nurse, and a doctor – a woman at that, I have nothing to say in my defence. During the final months I was strapped down at night and given medicine, pretty much as though I had been severely retarded.

That is over and done with long ago. There is no point in saying any more about it.

But before that happened I had started to read. The bit about the books really was true.

There was a visiting psychiatrist attached to the secure unit – a consultant, who had made a study of the connection between children's perception of time and their intelligence, at home and abroad. He talked about children in Ghana, where the people are Moors. How, even when they were in Primary VI or VII like me, they could not tell the length of a bus journey, whether it had taken ten minutes or six hours.

It was due to him that I was given books, although strictly speaking this ran counter to the treatment. What brought this about was that I had said I would like to read about time.

When Katarina had said that her mother and father had talked about time, I had instinctively known that there had to be books about it, that it must be possible to write about it.

At Lars Olsen's Memorial Home I saw and read for the first time books, given to me by the consultant, such as: E. J. Bickerman's *Chronology of the Ancient World*, Whitrow's *Natural Philosophy of Time*, and the *Guide to the History of Chronology*, vols I–III.

Back then I could not understand one word of what I read.

Reading did, however, give me heart. Even if you cannot understand what you are reading you can get something from books.

This was during the first weeks of my time there. When I worked on the speech, and felt that the work was progressing well.

It was Katarina who gave me the idea of doing it. Even though she was gone, still she was there.

Often she stood before me, even when I did not close my eyes. Her skin was so white – so transparent, almost – her sweater was too big and had belonged to her father who had hanged himself, her hair was tucked in at the collar. She had lured Baunsbak-Kold to the school and caused him to forget himself. And she had spoken to him. Unbidden, she had also spoken to Biehl and to Fredhøj.

Speaking is not easy. All your life you have listened, or looked as if you were. The living word came down to you, it was not something you, personally, gave voice to. You spoke only after having put up your hand, and when you had been asked a question, and you said what was certain and correct, what was beyond doubt.

With my speech the opposite was the case. It was full of uncertainty, and it was unbidden.

After a few weeks, I had to give up. Nor did I ever present it. When the confrontation came I was silent.

I have kept quiet ever since.

It was the child who made me aware that it was still not too late.

She was born in November 1990. In August 1991 I embarked upon this series of experiments in the laboratory. Now, as they approach their provisional conclusion, it is July 1993.

So she was not quite a year old when it began. Now, at its close, she is more than two and a half years old.

I started reading aloud to her from the manuscript when she was

197

eighteen months old. From the rest of the world I kept it strictly isolated. But I showed it to her. In the afternoons, when we were alone, I would take out the papers and read bits and pieces to her. At one point she then said that I ought to write the report, the unfinished speech.

I know that this statement will render me suspect. It will be asserted that she is, after all, just a little child and that what I am claiming is all but insane.

But it was she who suggested it.

There are many ways of suggesting something. It does not actually have to be put into words. You can sit quietly and listen and in this way show the other that what he is saying is all right. That he will not be judged. That you are his friend, no matter what.

One day she pointed out that it was not too late. After all, they were all still alive. There was still time to catch the boat.

Immediately, I understood. Biehl, Ærø and all the others who were present back then, they are still there, it is still not too late to have a word with them.

Until she showed me the way, I must have thought that it was over. I knew, of course, about Fredhøj and the stroke. But I had given up on the others too. It had seemed overwhelming, it was so long ago. When we had the chance of doing something, of saying something to them, only Katarina had the courage, and now it was, irrevocably, too late. In the laboratory I might be able to show a pale reflection of what took place. But, over the twenty-two years separating me from that time, I could not speak.

To this the child raised the objection that all of them were still around. Each and every one of the sixteen people who were present at the department's confrontation – Fredhøj excluded – are still around, that was what she said.

That the past is not over and done with. But that it lives on.

And so I prepared this.

IN DENMARK, two libraries have extensive collections of books on schools and education – the libraries at the Teacher Training College on Emdrupvej and at the Danish Institute of Education, which I have visited on a number of occasions.

I have looked for books on the history of education, I wanted to see what they wrote about time.

I found next to nothing. Next to nothing. *Pedagogikens historia, Education and Society in Modern Europe, Histoire mondiale de l'éducation, Schule und Gesellschaft, Skolen i Danmark*, next to nothing on time. And anything there might be amounts to facsimiles of timetables from previous centuries. They look just like what you have today, and they are not even commented on. Time plays no great part in books on the history of education, in a way it is not there at all.

In 1966, at the Academy of Sciences in New York, a society was formed for the purpose of studying time. It was given the name of the International Society for the Study of Time. The society held its first meeting in the Mathematisches Forschungsinstitut in Ober-wohlfalch, Dunkelwald, West Germany, in September 1969. G. J. Whitrow was elected president; J. T. Fraser, secretary, and most of the renowned theorists of time are members.

With all of them it is quite clear that they are on the inside. They are doctors and scientists, who have had no problems at school, but have grown up and flown out into the world.

You might wonder why, in the mid-1960s, an international society should be formed for the study of time; that their first meeting should be held in 1969, the year in which Biehl's first applications to the Ministry of Education are composed.

What you can be sure of is that this society is comprised of people who were always most diligent and precise.

Not that I want to speak ill of anyone. But I have my doubts as to how much such people can know about time. Or whether, about it, they can only know a few, specific things.

You might well doubt whether, in this society, it has ever made anyone ill.

And maybe you learn most about time if you have run up against it. If you have been ill and out on the borderline.

Theorists of time are seldom in agreement. However, they do agree that there are two possible ways of viewing the passage of time: that everything is in a state of constant and unrecognisable change. And that everything remains unchanged.

There it is, the supreme contradiction. Linear time and circular time.

Linear time has to be envisaged as a huge, endless knife-blade scraping its way across the universe, and drawing it along with it. In its wake it leaves an endless broad stripe of past time, ahead of it lies the future, on the knife-edge lies the present, in which we live.

Circular time sees the world as remaining more or less the same. With the changes around us being, or leading to, repetition.

These two perceptions of time have been almost predominant throughout history, up to our own century. Where a modified version of linear time is now said, by the experts, to be correct.

Both have been in existence for as long as the written word. Even though, far back, the linear theory is faint.

Far back there are the Ancient Egyptians. Biehl covered this civilisation in World History, shortly after I came to the school. He explained that it had been cruel but impressive; that, like the Roman Empire and the city state of Athens, it had fallen apart when it grew soft.

The same applied to the Mesopotamian civilisations which, in Biehl's lessons, succeeded the Egyptian, but now at a slightly higher level. It was in this way that civilisations succeeded one another, like children moving up a class each year.

It was quite evident from the teaching at Biehl's that these civilisations, along with Buddhism and Taoism, were precursors to our own time.

The experts still believe this. Right from *Guide to the History of Chronology*, vols I–III, published at the turn of the century, to Whitrow's *Time in History* from 1988, it is quite clear that the modern world's perception of time is far superior to that of the ancient world; that the history of the perception of time is like a plant that has grown slowly, blossoming only in this century. Or like a progressive function only now shooting up exponentially.

The experts have many different perceptions of time. But all are agreed on how things stand with their own field. It has been one long, linear triumph all the way up to the present day and the International Society for the Study of Time.

I believe that virtually all of the existing books on time, deep down, are certain that it is linear. That it passes and is then, irrevocably, gone.

Even with Bertrand Russell and Bergson, who have suggested so many other ways of perceiving time, you can sense that they only did it in jest. It has been like a game of chess. They have wanted to force their colleagues to play as well as possible. But they personally have never been in doubt. Even Einstein – in whose curved space-time there is no single time, but a fluid diversity of times running through the universe – even he can still write that, in local terms, time is linear.

Maybe they are wrong. Not meaning to speak ill of anyone, but maybe they are wrong.

I shall try to explain what I mean. In order to say it, I must first explain in more detail what I mean by linear and cyclic time.

*　　*　　*

The life of every person possesses a linear trait. All of us are born, grow up, live and end up being destroyed. In various ways, to be sure – some in holes in the ground, others in children's homes or at the Academy of Sciences in New York. But for each of us, birth, death and growing up are unique events that come round once, and once only, and can never be repeated – at any rate, not just like that. Their time is linear. As if you were moving along a straight line – each point you came past would be one you had never passed before and never would that same point come again.

And yet, life is full of repetition. Every day I install myself in the laboratory. This is the prerequisite for the experiment. If it is ever to be brought to a conclusion, this act must be repeated a great many times. In a way, time around the laboratory is cyclic.

So, too, with the body. Every second it dies a little, while still maintaining and regenerating itself. With every second it ensures the infinite regularity of breathing and pulse – rhythms which can still, at the same time, be altered, increase and culminate in fear and panic and ecstasy, only once more to seek equilibrium. And which now and then – when the woman and the child are nearby, or after working in the laboratory, or for some other reason – for fleeting moments, can result in cycles of perfect harmony; one steady, mathematically regular swing.

In the life of every person, on every conceivable plane, an uninter-rupted chain of both cyclic and linear traits can be found; identical re-enactments and unique, one-off occurrences.

There you have a contradiction in terms.

Read books about the history of time and you will find all of them agree that linear time triumphed along with Christianity. At any rate, from Augustine onwards Christ is most certainly dead, once and for all. Our repenting must be done here and now, there are no second chances, time is straight and irrevocable.

And yet, Kant is the first to speculate on how the Milky Way was created. And not until 1823 is an article stating that the universe is not static taken seriously. Even though linear time has triumphed, it is as though cyclic time is what counts.

This contradiction may have arisen because historiographers write about other historiographers. In the learned world of medieval Europe, in which most theories survived intact and side by side from the twelfth to the seventeenth centuries, time is linear.

While everyone else lived in a world which was, by and large, unchanging.

Thereafter, it has all come about in less than two hundred years. In 1865 Rudolf Clausius suggested the word "entropy" as a scientific term for the fact that time was linear, irrevocable, irreversible, and that nothing could ever be the same again.

Up to that point, even in biology, no one had really been sure of anything other than that living creatures kept on reproducing themselves; that nature was cyclic. Darwin's book on the origin of the species, on the survival of the fittest, constitutes the decisive break with the old way of thinking. After him, biological time is linear.

Because Darwinism is what carried the species forwards, towards increasingly complex organisms – micro-mutations, passed on through the normal process of reproduction. What drove the world forwards was the unique, the exceptions, the micro-mutations.

The everyday occurrence of having children and feeding them and bringing them up was nothing but a sort of vending machine for the norm, a beast of burden for mutants of a higher order.

In many ways, all of this has somehow fallen apart. Modern biology has had to consider the significance of the learning process, it has become impossible for it to explain everything, or even the greater part of it, by way of unique mutations. And physics seems to have gone quite to pieces, with no new theory lasting more than a couple of years. When I began work at Odense University most people believed that the superstrings theory could provide the definitive explanation of the secret of the universe. A year and a half later, when I had to stop work, the theory was definitively out of fashion, and already three-quarters abandoned. Today Hawking refers to it in *A Brief History of Time* as a small parenthesis in the history of physics.

Theories, therefore, enjoy ever briefer life spans and most die before they have the chance to grow up.

But not linear time. In a hundred and fifty years it has come to permeate everything. And still, now, as I write this, there seems to be nothing else.

Time at Biehl's Academy was absolutely linear.

It is almost impossible to explain. Because, at the same time, every day was the same. Every schoolday was like all the rest. Looking back at them, memory cannot distinguish between them.

Apart from those last months, after I met Katarina and August, and until we were separated for ever. That time you can never forget.

All the other days were alike. Actually, my schooldays were no different from my time in isolation. Apart from the fact that, at the latter establishment, I had no one to talk to and so reality went to pieces.

Otherwise there was no difference. The succession of days was an endless line, grey. They ran past you. Yourself, you were held firmly in place, you stood stock-still and watched them running past, and there was nothing to be done about it.

Maybe, somewhere inside you, you felt that surely it could have been otherwise. That it had not needed to be so hard and grey and monotonous. But you saw no way out. Until I met Katarina. But then, of course, everything fell apart.

When all the days were the same, when they recurred and recurred, and were planned out ten years into the future, why did you feel that time was passing, that it was linear, that your schooldays were a kind of countdown, that time was a train that you must and ought to be fit enough to hang on to?

I think it was because of the insistence on achievement. Otherwise it is impossible to explain.

* * *

Of course, it was only from the outside that the days seemed the same. Deep down they were meant to be different. It only seemed as though the same subjects and the same classrooms and the same teachers and the same pupils came round again and again. In reality, the requirement was that you should, with every day, be transformed. Every day you should be better, you should have developed, all the repetition in the life of the school was there only so that, against an unchanging background, you could show that you had improved.

I suppose that is why numbers were so important. I suppose that is why Biehl was so particular about the achievements in his memoirs, and why there were marks and timetables and endless files and summaries of people's pasts and proficiency and how many times they had been late. They saw the school as some divine ennobling machine. The numbers were proof and verification of its feasibility, its efficacy.

I know I cannot bring anyone to understand this. How our lives back then were totally saturated by time. Even those who were involved back then, even Biehl and Karin Ærø and all you others whom I have in mind, even you would deny it.

I believe we were on the outermost edge. I believe we were as far out as anyone can go with time. We were held down as tightly as anyone can be held down by a clock. So hard, in fact, that if your shell was not very thick, then you fell completely or partially to pieces.

I have felt that time ran in our veins like blood.

And if you became ill, if you cracked under time, then you were suffering from a disease of the blood.

Now and then – those nights when I lie awake, when I just listen to the woman and the child breathing – I grow frightened. And I fear that things may not have changed, out in the world; that time's grip will not have slackened.

I hope I am wrong. This is my greatest wish. To be utterly wrong.

Of course, there were schools elsewhere too, this I know. But surely no place with a vision such as Biehl's.

Elsewhere, in other countries, they have held children in the grip of time, for a while they have held them. But, in time, those children who could not cope, or whose parents did not have the wherewithal, were given up, dropped.

But Biehl would not give up on anyone, that was the exceptional thing – maybe the exceptional thing about Denmark. They would not entertain the thought that some pupils were down there, in darkness. They did not want to know anything about the darkness, everything in the universe had to be light. With the knife of light they would scrape the darkness clean.

It is as though that thought were almost insane.

$\cdot 3 \cdot$

THEY TOOK ME off the medicine gradually, over a week. It is
much harder to come off medicine than to go on to it. In all, over
those seven days, I did not sleep as many as eight hours.

The Department representative who collected me was accompanied by a policeman and an observer from child welfare services,
this was unnecessary, but they did not know what had taken place,
they felt insecure. I was also handcuffed.

It took place at the school. This was standard departmental practice – as close to the scene of the crime as possible.

In order to have enough room, they had had to take over a
classroom. In addition to Biehl, Karin Ærø and Fredhøj, and the
representatives from the Ministry of Education, Stuus was there –
as chairman of the board of teachers – along with two representatives from the parents' association, Aage Hårdrup, BD, Hessen,
Flakkedam, my guardian from the Children's Panel, Johanna Buhl,
the district medical officer, Astrid Biehl and a woman I had not
seen before, but who might have been the legal representative for
the Department of Health and Welfare. I counted sixteen people
altogether, plus Katarina and myself, the child-welfare representative and the policeman. It was said that the Director of Education
for Copenhagen, Baunsbak-Kold, should also have been there, but
had sent word that he was unavoidably detained.

They had positioned the desks so as to form a boxed-off compart-
ment on either side of the teacher's desk. Katarina and I stood, each
in our respective boxes, Biehl and Karin Ærø and Fredhøj sat over
by the wall, the Department representatives sat by the window,
with the light behind them. When the proceedings had been under
way for some time, Humlum came in, ever so quietly, and took a
seat in the back row.

207

The Department's representatives did most of the talking. They said this was not a trial or an inquisition, but merely an informal hearing, called to clear up certain points at issue.

They then summarised the background to the case – with which we were quite familiar. An experiment in the integration of defective children into ordinary schools which had now been abandoned, following what had occurred, but all particulars of which were still confidential. This last was directed at Katarina and myself. One sensed, in the room, a bitter, tense atmosphere – particularly between the school and the representatives of the Department. You were never told what had gone before. But one sensed that it must have been a disaster, Ragnarok.

First of all, they said, they were interested in hearing more about something that Peter – they meant me – had kept repeating, when questioned during his detention: that we had carried out an experiment. What was this about, what had I meant?

I did not remember having been questioned, to this very day I do not remember it, it must have been after the first three weeks of isolation, so I could not give them any answers. I was also having hot flushes, and spasms, after having come off the medicine. I stood with my arms folded to keep from shaking, but the desk I was leaning against still rocked. Nor was I used to so many people, they could see this and gave up on me.

Then they turned to Katarina. You would not have believed she could have become any paler, but she had. She had difficulty in talking. We had not seen one another for six months and eleven days, and yet I knew her as easily as though we were linked to one another, as though we were connected across time and space. As though we were twins, unborn twins linked together in their mother's womb.

You could see she did not blame me for having mentioned the experiment to them, she understood that I had been in isolation and pushed beyond time and reality, she had nothing bad to say about me, we were still friends. Even though she had maintained absolute silence for six months, and I, in a way, had betrayed us. All of this I saw in her face, before she answered them.

"I had discovered that there had to be different types of time," she said. "I discovered it when my father and mother died. Peter had seen it, too, we did research into the other types."

Everything went silent for a very long while, and in the silence they became convinced of what they had always known. That we were not in our right minds, not even she.

This she sensed.

"Let's just get it over with," she said.

It was like giving permission. That is how she was. Even among these people, at this moment, she could give permission.

Following her words, a sense of relief settled on the room. Now there was no more uncertainty. Now all doubt was gone. She had given them permission to cease doubting. We had been out of our minds, August, Katarina and me, this was the explanation. Not accountable.

Doubt was always the worst.

"What is most detestable," Biehl had said, "is when a child lies or conceals something."

In other words, when something is kept hidden, unclarified. That was the worst.

This was what I had tried to explain to Katarina, that night when we were sitting on her bed. That the whole school was like a device designed to remove doubt.

As with their experiment. They wanted to raise the incomprehensible, the dark and dubious children up into the light.

Subsequently I have discovered that it was not just Biehl. That it was not just our childhood, not just the early 1970s. Now I believe most of them were in on it, or all of those who wrote about time, from Augustine to Newton.

They have detested doubt.

In *Confessions* Augustine writes that time passes unprompted, regardless of man. He also says that it is linked to human perception. This is a contradiction, he offers no explanation, it is as though, for Augustine, there was nothing wrong with a bit of doubt here and there.

At the beginning of *Mathematical Principles of Natural Philosophy* Newton writes, twelve hundred years later, that "absolutely true, mathematical time flows according to its own nature, smoothly, unrelated to any external force."

Here there is no doubt. In fact, in all of *Mathematical Principles of Natural Philosophy* no doubt is shown of anything whatsoever.

What has happened, from Augustine to Newton, is that man has been removed from time. Now it passes whether man measures it or not, it has become objective. In other words, freed from human uncertainty.

But from then on there is disintegration, more or less. Newton is the last one who really believes in a time unconnected to man. Unconnected to things. Unconnected, come to that, to the universe.

Measurement of linear time gains ground in Europe. In real terms, it is only three hundred years old, everything else merely leads up to it. It appears when society begins to change so fast that each new day is no longer recognisable, because it has become too different from the day before. Time measurement appears as society grows more complex, it appears along with communications, the postal service, finance and trade, and with the railways.

For this, various explanations are given. It is said that time appears with the desire of the middle classes, together with science, to liberate themselves from the aristocracy and religion.

That, of course, is how it must have been, that must be a key element in the explanation. Whatever an explanation might be. But it is as though there is something else.

Reading Newton, not so much *Mathematical Principles of Natural Philosophy*, because in that he has so far removed man that even he – the author – is hardly there; as though the objective laws of nature, writing themselves, have produced the book; but in the letters, I think how much he has resembled Biehl. Their strictness, their need to remove all doubt, their ruthlessness. As though they are the same person, the same schoolmaster spanning three hundred years. As though time did not matter very much.

There must be something deeper and greater than the historical explanation. It is as though these scientists and philosophers, people with power and knowledge in Western civilisation, all have something in common. As though none of them could stand the darkness, did not want to know doubt and uncertainty. Were, within themselves, unable to cope with unresolved contradictions. And so they have tried to eliminate them.

Then, sooner or later, it has resulted in a breakdown.

We had been told that, at the school, we should look upon Karin Ærø – our class teacher – as our mother, and Biehl as our father.

That must have been why the Department had asked her. They had asked her to explain the school's point of view regarding the character of the relationship between Katarina and myself. August was not mentioned, but you understood what they were getting at. They had the idea that, somehow or other, we had driven him to it.

Karin Ærø had prepared a checklist of what they knew; a list of all the times we had been seen together, from when we were found, that first time, in the library during lessons, to when we had attempted to exchange information that did not concern us during the Advent morning service, and on until, on the night August died, we had been discovered locked in an embrace in the staff room.

She made no comment on the part about being locked in an embrace. But, when she said it, her voice changed. It was obvious that this was serious.

They knew so many things. Where and when we had been in contact with one another. Times and places. But of what mattered they knew nothing.

There were two from the Department, a man and a woman. The woman asked what we had to say to this. She addressed herself to Katarina, but I was the one who said something. I spoke to Biehl.

"What happened to August?" I said.

They tried to stop me, but I did not look at them, it was all I could do to keep my attention on Biehl. The only way of coping with so many people was to imagine a tunnel – I was at one end, Biehl was at the other, outside it there was nothing.

"How did you get out?" I said.

He gave an answer I had trouble hearing. I would have gone down to him, but I was attached to something – the policeman behind me, I had forgotten about him. I indicated to him that I needed my hands free, to demonstrate something. In the air I showed how one hand had a tight grip on the other.

"That's the kind of hold he had," I said, "you can't ever get out of that."

August had broken his fingers, such pain is too great for anyone to get away from. They did not understand me. Just Biehl.

"He let me go," he said.

"How did you get out?"

"By the door."

"It was bolted on the inside."

He stopped, and looked down at his hands. There was still something not quite right about two of the fingers, he was wearing his wedding ring on the other hand, the knuckles had become gnarled.

It was as though he was having difficulty remembering. Maybe he had needed to forget. So the memory had lodged in his hands. When he looked up his face was naked, as you had never seen it before. As though he were surprised and shaken by the question and, as well, by the answer he had to give me.

"He opened it for me," he said. "He must have repented."

I had asked something that touched very closely upon him and he had answered. That was the only time ever that such a thing occurred.

"He did not burn to death," said Katarina.

Just as she said it I thought that now she was going trot out the same story she had given about her parents. That her shell had not been thick enough after all, and now it was crushed.

"I spoke to the doctor," she said. "It was blisters on the inside of the windpipe."

There were three tunnels. Between her and Biehl and me. Everyone else was on the outside.

"He could have thrown it at you," she said to Biehl, "the bottle. But he let you go, he let you out. Then he threw it inside the room. And then he walked into the fire himself, and breathed in the flames. The blisters closed off his windpipe and he suffocated."

Everyone was very quiet. But I do not think they understood.

"It is as though time had gone backwards for him. Or as though the past had returned. He could have done it again. Killed someone."

She pointed at Biehl.

"But he didn't do it. He let you go. And then did away with himself. As though he had been given yet another chance."

JAKOB VON UEXKÜLL, a difficult name. Although it feels good to write it. I write in longhand, quite slowly.

I have a picture of him, taken from a newspaper. The face is a little heavy, very grave and yet somehow gentle.

Biehl had an MA in biology, yet he never mentioned Jakob von Uexküll, I do not think he had heard of him.

Uexküll was a professor of biology in Germany. During the 1920s and 1930s he wrote books and articles about the way in which living creatures perceived their surroundings, and particularly about their perception of time and space.

It is not difficult to read what he has written, not compared to some of the other books you fight your way through in your lifetime. At all times he has endeavoured to be very clear. And he has had nothing to hide, and if he has been in doubt then he has said so, straight out.

At the same time he is, in a way, humble. So humble that he believes that what he does is not so very different from what others before him have done. In the foreword to his book *Theoretical Biology*, he wrote that he was following the trail blazed by Helmholtz and Kant. They had insisted that it is impossible to perceive the reality that surrounds us – or to perceive ourselves – any way other than through the senses. And the senses are not passive receivers of reality, they process it. That which we perceive is heavily processed. So there is no point in talking about an actual reality, that outside of ourselves. That we have no knowledge of.

What we know is an edited version. Biology can concentrate on studying the way in which our sensory apparatus is constructed, how it edits. And how the consciousness of other living creatures operates as compared to our own.

Reading this for the first time, I thought that Uexküll must have stumbled upon the same thing as us, as Katarina and August and I, although in a better, more intelligent, way.

First we realised that there was a plan, later we came to understand it, just before everything fell apart.

Biehl's and Fredhøj's plan, covert though it might have been, was consciously acknowledged, they had defined it in their applications, it could be put into words. This was the plan for the grand integration, for the abolition of the darkness.

But behind this there was another purpose, greater, of which they knew nothing.

Never did we ask them about this purpose, not even Katarina. But if we had done, they would have replied that, beyond the school, beyond their plan, there was time. There was God.

They believed that, beyond the school, there was reality.

This cannot be true, even back then we sensed this. In what lay beyond the school, beyond their plan – especially time, which we felt flowing around us and saturating everything – there was a purpose. And in this greater purpose and plan we were, all of us, accomplices. In an absolutely inexplicable way, we were all working to create and maintain time at the school.

It was this that Jakob von Uexküll had written, in his own humble way, in the mid-1920s. We are not simply left to time. One way or another, it is also something we are constantly involved in creating.

Like a work of art.

If that really is the way of it, then it is important that people enter the laboratory every now and then, and ask questions of a different kind to those that are otherwise asked. If we are all maintaining time, then you have a place of your own, then it matters that you do something slowly, then even an experiment as transitory as this one can serve to touch time, in such a way that it will change.

*   *   *

How has time become like barbed wire? If we ourselves share the responsibility, how is it that it has closed in around us?

For this Uexküll has no explanation, nor could anyone expect one. He wrote about what he believed had to be the simplest building bricks of the sense of time – tempo, rhythm and the relationship between muscular action and sense of time. To study this was what he saw as his task, this was what he worked on in the laboratory. You can tell, from reading the very first pages, that he has done his best.

Even so you could not stay with him all the way. For that, people in his world are too alone.

Once you have realised that there is no objective external world to be found; that what you know is only a filtered and processed version, then it is a short step to the thought that, in that case, other people too are nothing but a processed shadow, and but a short step more to the belief that every person must somehow be shut away, isolated behind their own unreliable sensory apparatus. And then the thought springs easily to mind that man is, fundamentally, alone. That the world is made up of disconnected consciousnesses, each isolated within the illusion created by its own senses, floating in a featureless vacuum.

He does not put it so bluntly, but the idea is not far away. That, fundamentally, man is alone.

When, at Lars Olsen's Memorial Home, I had been isolated from other people for three weeks, the world ceased to exist. In fact, in the end, there was hardly any inner reality. If man becomes totally isolated then he ceases to exist.

So it is not fundamentally possible to be alone. Fundamentally, man has to be with other people. If man becomes totally, totally alone, then he is lost.

Johan Asplund, Swedish professor of social psychology, began, in his book *Time, Space, Individual, Collective* and in many other places, to examine the way in which time, as an entity, is maintained collectively by people. Just as Uexküll attempted to uncover the underlying rules for each individual's awareness of the world, so Asplund applies himself to describing the rules governing collective awareness, coexistence, in a way that no one has ever done before. And in a way, gently and modestly, like Uexküll.

The subject of his books is fellowship. Even so, in many ways they too stand alone.

Johan Asplund and Jakob von Uexküll. You read what they have written, and it is like a friend reaching out a hand to you, even though you will never get to meet them. They have known something special about time, maybe they themselves have been ill. They have known that there are limits to how tightly you can hold on to a person without them cracking.

Uexküll and Asplund: time is not something that flows independently of the individual and of human fellowship. It is also shaped and maintained by the way people coexist, and this is linked to the sensory apparatus.

When the bell rang the woman from the Department got to her feet and looked at her watch.

"I think we've reached the end of the road," she said.

The end of the road. It was so deep. She meant that it was now clear that we – not August alone, but also Katarina and I – had not been accountable. That it was impossible to get any further by spending more time on it. That they had covered the distance they had set for themselves. That they had punished Biehl and the school enough by putting a stop to the project.

She also meant that the time was right for terminating the proceedings at this point. The bell had rung. As though urging that the confrontation ought to come to a close.

Everyone stood up, including Biehl and Fredhøj and Karin Ærø and all the others, even grown-ups who had not gone to school for thirty years. It was a reflex. The moment the bell rang, time began to flow. It would carry everything with it, out of the room.

Against this stream, all hunched up, came Katarina. They did not try to stop her, but they froze. She came right over and stood in front of me.

I thought she was going to say something about the experiment, that it continued for always, that it never stopped, and then I would have nodded.

But it was not that.

"I'm going to Svarrø," she said. "It'll only be for a few months. I'll leave an address for you."

If you belonged nowhere, and if you became separated from one another, then it was as though you ceased to exist, even in a country as small as Denmark; then you never found one another again, this I had witnessed often before, this she knew.

She looked up at me, her face was screwed up. With love. I could not stand it.

"I'll come, you'll see," I said. I knew it was a lie, she knew it too.

If it had just been her and me. But there had always been August too, now he was obliterated, it was as if you had lost your own child, I could no longer see her.

When people are going to be taken from you anyway, then it would be better if you had never come to care for them.

"Try to remember the bit about the pain," she said. "And the light of awareness."

No one laid a hand on her. But the stream of time grabbed hold of her and carried her out and away.

5

WHAT DOES IT MEAN, to fail a child?

Over the years that I have been writing this, Princeton University, where Einstein held a post, has embarked on the publication of his collected works. The first volume contains his correspondence with Mileva Mariø, his first wife.

In November 1901 they had a daughter, Lieserl, out of wedlock. Eight months later they gave her away in adoption, possibly to a family in Hungary. Most likely because she stood in the way of Einstein's appointment, and his career. At that time Mileva Mariø was once more pregnant. The whole affair was kept secret. No one, subsequently, could find any trace of Lieserl, the only clue to her existence lies in these letters.

Most of Einstein's letters from this time, including those in which he enquires after the daughter, follow the same pattern: a few lines taken up by enquiries about mother and child, after which he immediately switches to news of what really occupied his mind. During these years, mostly questions on thermodynamics; questions which were to lead, not long afterwards, to that particular theory of relativity, published in 1905, in which he propounds the first part of his theory on time.

He was divorced from Mileva Mariø in 1919, by which time they had had a son. The rift lasted until the late 1920s, after which they resumed the relationship, as friends. From the next twenty years, several hundred of the letters they exchanged have been preserved.

In these the daughter given up for adoption is not mentioned once, not even in the spaces between the lines.

What causes people to abandon a child? And what impact will it later have on them, that they have done so?

*   *   *

When Einstein has become world famous, and journalists ask about his youth, he himself refers to it several times as *"the corpse of my childhood"*.

He says he is referring to the strict, inhibiting bourgeois mentality that surrounded him.

It is clear from his letters to Mileva Mariø that his scientific theories are developed in protest against this bourgeois mentality, which he also encounters at his Swiss Polytechnic.

He himself has later said that for him the theory of relativity and its view of time and space was also an act of rebellion against authorities that inhibit thought. In his letters it is quite clear that his cosmology has also been developed as political action and psychological protest.

Like a strategy for survival. Some ate frogs, others developed, in the laboratory, a theory of the universe.

At the same time, the inhibition he protested against in his work, the narrow-mindedness, is what causes him and Mileva Mariø to give away their eight-month-old daughter.

"The corpse of my childhood."

For twenty years I purposely refrained from thinking of Katarina. If the thought occurred unbidden, I turned away from it. It was the child who persuaded me to leave off doing this. It happened in the autumn of 1991, at which time I had only been writing this for a few months. She came to me in the laboratory: "You still have to track down Katarina," she said.

Not outright, not in words, but still brooking no denial.

She, the child that is, thinks very little about the past, and hardly at all about the future. Her attention is taken up by the space and objects and people around her at this moment. This makes you look at yourself.

If you lived like that and, like her, never thought about the future, then it would be hard to achieve what was expected of you, then you would find it hard to cope with the practicalities. Especially since, around you, everything is planned out, perhaps not ten years into the future like at Biehl's, but still far ahead.

But if you are too afraid of the future, or if your thoughts are drawn back to disasters that are, in any case, over and done with, then you become impotent. When this happens, I just sit and look at her. From the present she calls to me, but I cannot help her, I have been drawn back into the past and regret, or forwards into fear of what is to come. I am in another time and in it I am worth nothing to her.

She, however, has helped me. I have looked at her, watched her playing, I try to learn to do as she does, or at least something along the same lines.

She made me aware that I still had to see Katarina. That, in the long run, struggling against the past to keep it at bay is exhausting.

Even so, I put it off for months. It was winter when I went to Svarrø. There was barbed wire around the building, and a barrier manned by a security guard. I was not allowed in, he spoke on the phone to the office, the staff had all changed since that time, he said, no one who was there now could remember anything about it.

As I was leaving he said that the old superintendent lived down in the village.

It was a little house, dark, seeming to lie in the shadow of the treatment home – even though it was a kilometre away and out of sight. Why had they stayed there?

He sat in an armchair, smoking a pipe. Behind him, in silence, stood his wife. I had left my shoes in the hall, I stood there in my stockinged feet, they did not invite me to sit down.

"Are you related?" he said.

"I went to school with her."

"We're sworn to secrecy," he said.

"She's been left something in a will. The executors are offering a reward of a thousand kroner."

Something passed between them, wordlessly and without him turning round. Then he made an effort to remember. So many years and so many children, one year and one child barely distinguishable from the next. But he tried. To achieve something and be deemed worthy.

221

"She was discharged and removed in 1972, this much is certain. The secure unit had been set up three months earlier. After the accident. We had been ordered to take in boys too – up till then we had only had girls. She was raped and almost strangled."

I counted out the money on to a low card-table covered in green baize.

"Where did she go?"

"You forget after a while," he said. "She got out, I suppose."

"Out where?"

The question puzzled him.

"Just out. Set free."

On the way out, Biehl stopped in front of me. He wanted to say something, but he could not. He, who was known as a great speaker.

I think it was the first time he really looked at me. Until then he had seen me as a grey shadow, in the stream of pupils. Now he saw me as a person. His customary self-control had left him, his face reflected what he saw. A wretch, a borderline case, a confirmed liar. And yet, a human being.

I am probably wrong. But it was as though he wanted to ask something of me.

Forgiveness had always been an important word at the school. It had been important to Grundtvig, it was important to Biehl. If a pupil committed an offence he either meted out punishment or he let it pass. In both cases, however, the aim was a state of forgiveness.

But it had always been from them that the forgiveness had come, from God to them and then on to us. They felt that time was on their side; that not only had they themselves long been forgiven, they had also been chosen.

And yet it was as though that was what he was asking me for. Forgiveness. But I was probably wrong.

6

FOR TWENTY YEARS I refrained from seeking out Katarina. When at last I did so, at the child's request, she had disappeared leaving no address.

But I have not given up. I know she is out there somewhere. She will read this, and understand it more deeply than any other living person. She will read it and it will be clear to her that never since what happened back then have I stopped trying to touch time and see it change.

Then she will seek me out. She will meet the woman and the child and like them. If she does not have a family of her own we will tell her that she can stay as long as she likes, no one here expels anyone. Ragnarok is past.

Then I will show her the laboratory.

Ragnarok. We learned about it, they said it was the end. The end of the world, total obliteration.

As an adult I read it for myself, and saw that they had been wrong. There was, after all, an afterlife.

It is there in the prophecy of the Völuspa, the Elder Edda. There it says that the gods lay on the grass in the sun and played a game, the pieces were of gold, it was brilliant. Then came the war between the light and the dark, disaster, total obliteration.

But afterwards the gods were lying there in the light again, as before, playing with the gold pieces.

As though death and war and defeat had not been the final act after all, but merely a new beginning. As though, for the gods, time was one long process of repetition.

As though, after Ragnarok, there was yet another chance.

To have yet another chance.

The child is my chance, the third. When she looks at me, directly and at length and without judging, then it is as though she is the adult and I am a child, and she is making sure that nothing bad shall befall me. Or as though I am grown up and she is me as a child – but a child who, this time, is protected by its parents, as you yourself never were, or no, it is impossible to explain, but she is my third chance.

The first was when Karen and Erik Høeg found me, at Sandbjerg-gård, and adopted me in 1973 when I was fifteen years old. For this I will be eternally grateful to them. Without this I would have been obliterated.

The second chance is the woman.

The laboratory, here, is the fourth chance.

When you are given yet another chance, time goes backwards, the past returns. Then, yet again, you go through whatever it was that led to disaster. But this time there is hope.

"Farthest back you remember a plain," she said. "It is from the days before time enters your life, in other words you have lived without time, the way small children do."

This she said on the telephone, when we had been separated totally.

Farthest back I remember the Christian Foundation. The garden, the bathroom, the reading of Thought for the Day from the *Christian Daily*. These memories are not in any sequence, they lie on the timeless plain of my childhood. From there I sank downwards, maybe I was born to sink, maybe this was the covert Darwinism.

There was some slight upward movement, like my succeeding in getting to Crusty House and then to Biehl's. But, in the main, I sank.

This lasted until Katarina and August and I were brought together in time and space. Since then I have never completely lost heart.

*　　　*　　　*

To begin with, after the confrontation, I was sent back to Lars Olsen's Memorial Home. They were concerned. If I had been strong enough I would have reassured them. I was just hibernating, I had retreated, downwards and inwards, to a quiet place. At Crusty House, Oscar Humlum put his frogs – the ones he would make his money from, by eating them – at the very bottom of the vegetable drawer where the kitchen girls would not find them. Under the leeks, where the temperature was just above freezing point. There they did not die, they fell into a deep, motionless winter sleep, they waited for the light. If you took them out and let them lie on your hand, they stretched out towards the warmth and came to life.

We met – Katarina, August and I – and from then on it became impossible ever again to give up completely. I have given some thought to why this should be.

I believe it was love. When once you have encountered it, you will never sink again. Then you will always yearn for the light and the surface.

Twice I have seen Biehl in the street, Copenhagen is not that big.

He has grown grey, like stone. He still walks briskly and purposefully, although his sight does not seem to be so good.

The thought crosses your mind that he has aged like a caricature of Uexküll's theory: a lonely man, behind an unreliable sensory apparatus, in an unreal world.

When this is finished I will give it to him. I will find him, stand in front of him and give it to him.

"Back then I said not a word. Now I have said it."

There exists a time-lapse so lengthy that science finds it impossible to conceive of anything greater. This – 2×10^{17} seconds – is the time taken by a ray of light to traverse the conjectured radius of the universe. It is known as *the cosmic chronon*.

There exists a space of time so brief that it is impossible to calculate with anything less. This – 10^{-23} seconds – constitutes the irreducible minimum for the attribution of significance to regular processes. It is known as *the atomic chronon*.

It is thought that there exists also an upper and a lower *mental chronon*, that delimits the minimum and maximum time that consciousness can span.

If one is fit, then this is of no great interest, then you have no problem sharing time with other people.

But if one becomes unwell, and if time starts to float, then you run into the mental chronon.

When Biehl had struck – hard, deliberately and at the same time senselessly – there was a very brief pause. It was too brief to be noticed, it lasted less than one mental chronon, it was there, and then it was past, and only traces were left. A vague fear you did not understand.

But if you were ill, then you sensed this moment. That was precisely what we had, a pathologically heightened sensitivity to very brief spaces of time. Then you saw all of the endless and complex intimations of power contained in that instant; saw, too, how all of those present were left with a subtle, everlasting stamp of fear, and how this had to do with learning about time.

7

UEXKÜLL SAID THAT man is not that much better than a spider.

A spider's sight and hearing are poor and its sense of smell is not that great either, which means that its surroundings are limited by its sensory apparatus. But it has its web, by means of which it has extended its sensibility far beyond itself. Its sense of touch is very acute, by every movement of the web it can judge how far off and how big.

In the mornings at the Christian Foundation, when you crept out into the garden before anyone else was awake – not even the sisters – spiders' webs hung between the bushes. Drops of dew clung to the strands, they caught the sun. And if you touched the web, even quite gently, the spider would not appear. You had wanted to trick it into showing itself, but its sensitivity was so much greater than your own, it knew you were too big and powerful. Even though you were quite small.

Man is not that much better than a spider, says Uexküll.

The biggest webs were maybe seventy-five centimetres in diameter. Plus the strands to the tree trunks to which they clung. We had an agreement that no one was allowed to break the web, it was a rule among the children, the web was so big and the spider so small, you knew how it must have slogged to make it.

Sister Ragna, who looked after the garden, swept it down with a broom. When she did this, things always went very still, so dead still that she always stopped short and looked around. She could not understand it, all these children suddenly standing absolutely motionless.

During these moments she was in imminent peril of her life. Only a few details, the difference between her body weight and ours, the fact that the office on the first floor directly overlooked the garden, prevented us from obliterating her.

The webs were so perfect. So regular and yet irregular. Totally identical and always different. Infinitely.

And almost never bigger than seventy-five centimetres.

Through its web the spider did not sense the whole world. It sensed only that part of it that the web could pick up. Direction, distance, maybe the approximate weight of its quarry, maybe its size. But certainly not much more.

Thus, too, with science and its twin, industrial technology. Physics extends its web out into the universe or down into matter, and thinks it is discovering ever greater slices of reality.

It might be feared that this is a fallacy, that is what Uexküll was on the verge of believing. If the spider extended its web further, beyond the seventy-five centimetres, it would still only be able to sense what lay in its own and the web's nature to sense. It would not find a new reality. It would discover more of what it already knew. Of what lay beyond – colours, birds, smells, moles, people, sisters, God, the trigonometric functions, measurement of time, time itself – it would still be hovering in absolute ignorance.

That is the one thing I wanted to say.

The other is this: maybe it is possible to put it in stronger terms than Uexküll. Maybe the spiders at the Christian Foundation were smarter than man. Because they never extended their webs beyond a certain limit.

What would have happened if they had done so? If the spider's web were extended to infinity, as far out across and down under the threshold of the human sensory apparatus as technology has extended its sensors?

What would have happened is this: pretty soon the spider would be unable to cope physically with inspecting everything that became caught in the web. And if the web kept on extending, farther and farther away, then the spider would start to receive signals from areas inhabited by other insects and with a climate other than its own. And it would receive many more signals than it could deal with. Then the abnormally large web and what it brought back would come into conflict with the essence of the spider, with its nature.

While the web would begin to change the world around it. Maybe it would become too heavy, maybe finally it would crash to the ground, dragging great trees with it in its fall. Maybe it would take the spider with it into perdition.

This is the other thing I have wanted to say: man's exploration of the world, its web, also changes this world. When I lie awake at night, when I cannot sleep and I sit up and look at the child and the woman, then I am afraid, then I know that the web has extended far too far beyond the sensory apparatus. Now it is reaching out to black holes and stellar nebulae, and down to elementary particles that grow ever smaller, it is discovering things that then rebound onto everyday life, becoming refrigerators, schoolbooks, caesium clocks, submarines, computers, car engines, atom bombs and a steady increase in the pace of life.

In 1873, at the meridian conference, when Sandford Fleming of the Canadian Pacific Railway suggested a "universal world time" for the entire globe, America had seventy-one different time systems. In 1893 the American version of Fleming's initiative was raised to the status of law in Germany. Just after the turn of the century large sections of Europe switched to Greenwich Mean Time.

Man extended time as an instrument right across the world. And into the education of children the school extended precision and accuracy. So far, that they reached the limits of what human beings can bear. The limit at which the web starts to yield to its own weight. And to pull the spider with it in its fall.

We never tore down or split a web at the Christian Foundation. You looked at it and you understood that it was an expression of balance. The spider had done what it could. The web was fine as it was.

Was the spider familiar with time?

For a long time, whenever Sister Ragna had swept away the web, no new one was spun at the same spot. It was as though the spiders sensed the future. Animals do, I suppose. I suppose they retain an approximate memory of what has happened and learn from it. And they can anticipate what will happen in the not too distant future. They know how events follow one another. They must have some awareness of succession.

But that is not time, is it? Time means sensing that behind those changes which are an expression of time, there is fellowship.

When we say "time", I believe we mean at least two things. We mean changes. And we mean something unchangeable. We mean something that moves. But against an unmoving background. And vice versa.

Animals can sense changes. But consciousness of time involves the double sense of constancy and change. Which can only be attributed to those who give expression to it. And that can only be done through language, and only man has language.

The perception of time and language are inextricably bound up with one another.

If we say that "time has passed", then something must have changed – if nothing else, then the position of the hands on a clock, otherwise we would not know that anything had passed. At the same time something must have remained the same – if nothing else, then time itself, otherwise we could not recognise the new situation as something that has sprung from the starting point. The word "time" contains a unity of movement and changelessness.

The life of every person contains something of significance. You may not be all that well fitted, but no matter. The significant factor is human nature. Against it you can perpetrate a fair amount of violence, but if it becomes too much, then you are destroyed.

It is as though science has felt that human nature was something within which you were confined. Like being in detention on a red warrant. And so they have tried to push against it, as though to break out. And then it has all gone wrong.

At Biehl's you had to sit down for five to six hours every day – not

230

including compulsory prep – five days a week plus Sunday for the boarders, over forty weeks a year, for ten years. While constantly having to strive to be precise and accurate, in order to improve.

I believe that this went against the nature of children.

There could be a veil of mist in the mornings at the children's home, a white smoke ascending from the earth. At the point where it met the sunlight from heaven, dewdrops hung in the spider's web – big with curved, reversed reflections of the white strands and the misty grass and your own face. As though small globular universes were being born where the water from the earth met the fire from heaven. And somewhere in the silent beauty of these curved, looking-glass worlds you recognised yourself because of the crew cut.

The web, the light, the dew, all of this must have been part of the spider's world and its nature. But not as a limitation, not like isolation. We did not see it that way back then, and I have never, later on, been able to see it that way. Nature is not a straitjacket that must be burst open. Nature is a blessing, an opportunity for growth that has been bestowed upon all living things.

Like a guideline in your life.

To Plato, God was a mathematician. To Kepler, too, and to Biehl and Fredhøj. I do not believe it was a coincidence that their main subjects were biology and mathematics. A purpose behind them, the purpose that steered both them and the school, had caused them to align their own fates as closely as possible with God.

Mathematics is a kind of language. The only one in the universe that spurns the thought of limits.

Under duress, psychology and biology have admitted that there is a limit to the conditions to which living creatures may be subjected. That there is a limit to the amount of discipline, hard work and firm structure that children can bear.

Even physics has its limits. The cosmic and the atomic chronon. The upper and the lower limit.

But mathematics is limitless. Because there are no lower and upper limits, there is only infinity. Maybe this, as they say, is in itself neither bad or good. But there, where we met it – as a manifestation of time, as figures measuring achievement and improvement, as an argument for the feasibility of the absolute — it was not human. It was unnatural.

Fredhøj and Biehl never said it straight out, but I know now, with certainty, what they were thinking. Or maybe not thinking, but sensing. What that cosmology was, upon which all of their actions rested. They were thinking that in the beginning God created heaven and earth as raw material, like a group of pupils entering Primary I, designated and earmarked for processing and ennoblement. As the straight path along which the process of evolution should progress He created linear time. And as an instrument for measuring how far the process of evolution had advanced, He created mathematics and physics.

I have had the following thought: what if God were not a mathematician? What if He had been working, like Katarina and August and me, without actually having defined either questions or answers? And what if His result had not been exact, but approximate? An approximate balance perhaps. Not something that had to be improved upon, a springboard to further achievement, but something that was already more or less complete and in equilibrium. Like two trees and the sun and the moisture from the earth, between which all you had to do was to spin your web to the best of your ability, and that would have been enough, no more would be expected. And if any development should take place, then it would take place partly by itself, there would be no need for you to achieve anything extreme, you could just remain true to your nature, and it would take place. Now what if that were the intention?

August and Oscar Humlum and Katarina have paid me visits.

There are many ways of putting in an appearance and being heard without turning up in person.

Now I will say it. What I, personally, believe about time.

*　　*　　*

To sense time, to speak about time you have to sense that something has changed. And you have to sense that within or behind this change there is also something that was present before. The perception of time is the inexplicable union in the consciousness of both change and constancy.

In peoples' lives, in yours and mine, there are linear time sequences, with and without beginnings and endings. Conditions and epochs that appear with or without warning, only to pass and never come round again.

And there are repetitions, cycles: ups and downs, hope and despair, love and rejection, rearing up and dying away and returning again and again.

And there are blackouts, time-lags. And spurts of time. And sudden delays.

There is an overwhelmingly powerful tendency, when people are gathered together, to create a common time.

And in between all of these, every conceivable combination, hybrid and intermediate state is to be found.

And, just glimpsed, incidences of eternity.

When I was isolated for a long time, or had stopped talking, or got brushed by the train, or lay and waited for Valsang, or sat close to Katarina, or held August's hand, then time faded away, like a sound growing fainter. When I was heading away from the world and into my self, or in death or surrender or ecstasy, or in the silence here in the laboratory, then time departed from me. Then eternity drew near.

Time is inextricably bound up with language, with the sensory apparatus, and with human fellowship. Time comes into being when the mind encounters the world in a normal life.

Without contradicting anyone I would like to take issue with Newton who thought that time runs through the universe regardless of man, and with Kant who thought that time is inborn in the mind. I believe that time is a possibility inherent in all people at all times, but that teaching is required if it is to unfold, and whatever shape

233

it takes will depend upon the character of the teaching and the environment.

Time is a sphere made up of language, colours, smells, senses and sounds, a sphere in which you and the world coexist, an instrument with which to put the world in order and comprehend it, one of the reasons for your survival.

But if time grows too tight, then it becomes a reason for doing away with yourself.

Time is not an illusion. Nor is it the only reality. It is one possible, widespread form for encounters between the mind and the surrounding world. But not the only possible one. If you are driven by curiosity, or if you are ill and cannot survive any other way, then you can enter the laboratory and touch time. And then it will change.

You could let your mind go blank in front of a dewdrop, and time stood still. You could be waiting to have your head shoved down the toilet and time went too fast, and yet not fast enough. You could remember things from last year as if it were today and fear something from tomorrow as if that too were today. And you could have gone with Oscar Humlum for a weekend at the holiday home for underprivileged children at Høve, because they did not know what should be done with us and there was just him and me, no one supervised us; we swam, suddenly two days had passed and where had they gone?

The problem does not arise until language and society and development and science and school and we ourselves demand a choice, demand one truth. The development of the past three hundred years has required linear time.

Linear time is unavoidable, it is one way of hanging on to the past. Like points on a line – the Battle of Poitiers, the Black Death 1347, Columbus discovering America, Luther at Wittenberg, the beheading of Struensee 1772. And what I am writing here, this part of my life, is also remembered in this way.

But it is not the only way. The mind also remembers stretches, fluid passages, connections between what has once happened and what is happening now, regardless of the passage of time. And farthest back, the mind remembers a timeless plain.

If you grow up in a world that only permits and rewards one form of memory, then force is being used against your nature. Then you are imperceptibly nudged out towards the edge of the abyss.

Time is made up of many different states of consciousness, of symbols from human life.

This means that time is also a sphere of language, like a landscape, the place you make for when you try to comprehend, in particular, those elements in the world concerned with its change.

Like all linguistic landscapes time is not just a matter of words or linguistic significance. It is also colours, tones, rhythms, touch, tension, relaxation and scent.

In its simplest form it is the indescribable combination of recognition and surprise that arises when the mind encounters the movement of the world. It is the acknowledgment of the fact that, in every change, there is something never before seen, something unique and irreversible, and something that always remains the same.

Time refuses to be simplified and reduced. You cannot say that it is found only in the mind or only in the universe, that it runs in only one direction, or in every one imaginable. That it exists only in biological substructure, or is only a social convention. That it is only individual or only collective, only cyclic, only linear, relative, absolute, determined, universal or only local, only indeterminate, illusory, totally true, immeasurable, measurable, explicable or unapproachable. It is all of these things.

You see, for you, yourself, life is in fact irrevocable. When your problems were so great that they piled up until finally you could only see yourself – or not even that – then life ran away from you, through your fingers, like sand.

But if you stand back from yourself, for example because the child helped you, then you see the repetition: then you begin to see that you are only one transitory link in chains of almighty circuits; that you were not, after all, important, not because you were worthless – you were not, even though you were small you were important – but because the great repetitions are so much bigger and more important.

If your mind only senses itself, then it only sees the irrevocable time. But if it sees the family and heredity and the children and the births and being with others, then it sees the repetitions, then time is not so much an hourglass – its sand slipping away and running out – as a stretch, a plain, a continent you can journey across.

I have woken in the night, the child has kicked off her duvet, I do not know whether she has been too warm or has been afraid of being hemmed in. I have laid the duvet across her legs alone, that way at least she will not be cold and if she becomes desperate she can free herself in a second. Then I have not been able to get back to sleep, I have sat in the dark and looked at them both, the child and the woman. And the feeling has become too much. It is not sorrow or joy; it is the weight and the pressure of having been brought into their lives, and of knowing that if one were ever to be separated from them, it would mean your obliteration.

Then I have prayed. Not to anyone, God and Jesus will always be too close to Biehl, but out into the universe, to that place where the grand plans are formed, including those that lay behind and above Biehl's and our time there. I have prayed for our survival. Or at any rate for that of the child and the woman.

I believe that Biehl's Academy was the last possible point in three hundred years of scientific development. At that place only linear time was permitted, all life and teaching at the school was arranged in accordance with this – the school buildings, environment, teachers, pupils, kitchens, plants, equipment and everyday life was a mobile machine, a symbol of linear time.

We stood on the edge, we had reached the limit. For how far you could, with the instrument of time, push human nature. And then it was bound to go wrong.

FROM THE CONFRONTATION they drove me back to Lars Olsen's Memorial Home. I stayed there for fourteen days, but not in isolation. On the fifteenth day my guardian from the Children's Panel came to see me.

She told me that the school and the police had wanted to hold a judicial enquiry, into possible grounds of complicity in a violent act and driving one or possibly more schoolfellows to suicide. They had also unearthed the bit about Humlum. She and the child-welfare people had opposed them, they had pointed out my age – paragraph 15 of the penal code for 1930. Regardless of the enquiry's outcome I would have ended up under the Department of Health and Welfare, this she had made them aware of.

We were alone while we talked, she had sent the duty officer away, she had never been afraid of me. She looked tired, she was guardian to two hundred and eighty children, this she had told me.

She had saved the worst till last, not until she was at the door did she bring herself to say it.

"You're going to Sandbjerggård," she said.

"What about Katarina?"

At first she did not understand.

"The girl? We got her away from them, too. Even though she is over fifteen. 'Charge conditionally withdrawn.' Administration of Justice Act, paragraphs 723 and 723a."

The state-approved school of Sandbjerggård, primarily for mildly retarded and backward adolescents, was situated near Ravnsborg. August had been there for a short time before coming to Biehl's. Those who had been given up on, or who were too young to be

238

put in a proper prison, or in the unit for the exceptionally dangerous and criminally insane at the State Hospital at Nykøbing, Zealand, were sent there. The home had sixty residents and the same level of security as Herstedvester Prison – guards, towers, seven-metre high double fence with barbed wire. Even so people frequently ran away, one or two at a time – although never planned like at Himmelbjerg House. Unfocused. They stayed out for two days at the most. The second time it happened while I was there they had committed several rapes. A demonstration was staged outside the gate by people from the area, they carried shotguns and pickaxes. We hid in the grass and watched them, they had written placards, one of them said they should bring back the death penalty.

Workshop training was given in heavy industrial work, particularly metalwork. No one really took it seriously, not even the teachers, no one expected people to manage in any reasonable manner on the outside. Over half were receiving mandatory psychiatric treatment, many were checked up on by child welfare and the vice squad on a weekly basis.

In the long run, you can never be any better than your surroundings. When you are in the company of people who look down upon themselves as though they were animals, you too become like an animal. Or worse, because animals do not despise themselves.

We cut out steel plates. They came already primed, two metres by one and a half metres and twenty-five millimetres thick. We cut them with a big cutting blade fitted to the grinder, so the safety cover cannot be used, a shower of sparks flies back over your arms. One day I had taken my gloves off and rolled up the sleeves of my boiler suit and had started cutting with my arms bare. The iron filings burned a black worm up to the elbow, the burnt flesh stank. At first I did not feel anything, I had not known what I was doing, another person inside me had taken over. To make me sense the numbness that had settled over me.

That evening I did not go into the television room, I sat out in the toilets and wrote a letter to my guardian, saying that I needed to see her, and would she come as soon as it was convenient.

*   *   *

She came the next week. There were no female staff at Sandbjerg-gård, when she walked across the forecourt people hung out of the windows and opened their trousers and shouted at her.

There was a visiting room; she sent the officer out.

"I want to be adopted," I said.

First she went absolutely quiet.

"You're fourteen years old," she said.

If orphans were not adopted as babies, because they were too ugly, or gave the impression of being brain damaged, or for other reasons, then no more was ever said to them about adoption. And you never brought up the subject yourself.

I suppose, actually, you were afraid of the family. You knew you were unfit.

But now I had met August and Katarina. I would never have been able to explain it to Johanna Buhl. But if you have once sensed that someone cares for you, then you will never sink again.

"It's what I want," I said. "What are the conditions?"

"It has to go through the National Council for the Unmarried Mother and her Child," she said. "They have an adoptions office in Copenhagen. According to recommendations from the select committee for the Department of Health and Welfare, and that of the National Council for the Unmarried Mother and her Child, it has been the practice to investigate the child's situation, and that of the natural parents and the prospective adoptive parents. In a case such as yours, where it will be said that there may be some doubt as to the state of the child's mental health, you will have to be examined by a specialist, just as it will be necessary to obtain a statement from the Institute for Genetic Studies, as to whether you have a predisposition towards any hereditary illnesses, it's all there in White Paper number 262 from 1960. And then comes the problem of finding someone who will have you. The National Council for the Unmarried Mother holds weekly conferences which are attended by a psychiatrist, a psychologist, a paediatrician, a lawyer and a social worker. Statements will also be obtained from those institutions in which you have been placed. The statement from your last place, Biehl's Academy, will be particularly, and absolutely, crucial. So perhaps you should just forget the whole thing."

You could not make outside calls from Sandbjerggård. Some of the inmates had abused and tormented little girls, and after they had been taken into custody they had continued to call the girls at home. After that all the telephones were disconnected, now you could only make calls from a locked box while an officer listened in.

I called Biehl's Academy, the secretary answered the telephone, when I gave my name she went very quiet.

I apologised for ringing, but there were some things which had been left behind in my room and which I missed very much. She said she would forward them. Yes, I said, but there was also something concerning what had happened which I would like to say, would it be possible for me to speak to someone in authority?

It was Fredhøj who came. He parked his Rover in the forecourt, no one shouted at him.

He was very curt in the visiting room. As far as he was concerned I had ceased to exist.

While I was in isolation, my own clothes had been returned to me – two pairs of trousers, two cord shirts, underwear, socks, a sweater, a raincoat. What Fredhøj brought were personal effects that had been in my locker – slippers, gym shoes, PE kit, satchel and pencil case. There should also have been some cartoon books and a Stiga table-tennis bat. They were not there, I did not mention them, they must have been stolen the day after I was taken away, the contents of the pencil case too – it was quite empty. I said nothing either about the stitching of the satchel having been slit open, whoever had done it had tried to repair it, albeit clumsily, so I said nothing.

In addition, Fredhøj had brought me three books, the only three that, as a pupil, you had to purchase for yourself and therefore owned. Mine had been paid for by the social services department who had bought them second-hand. The books were: *Primary and*

Lower-Secondary Biology, *A Pocket Flora* and *The Folk High School Song Book*.

More times than you could remember Fredhøj had questioned you, up at the blackboard. Or you had sat and listened while he read stories about the great criminals. I had been in the class when Anne-Dorthe Feldslev found Axel in the chart locker. And yet now it was all he could do to look at me.

It was not indifference, it was distaste.

"I want to be adopted," I said. "I can't stay here, I'm going insane. Do you think I could have a statement from the school to the effect that I am fit to be with a family?"

He opened the door, the officer came in and signed a receipt on my behalf for the clothes and books. When you were in care you could not sign for yourself until you were sixteen. Not until he had gone out and closed the door did Fredhøj answer.

"No one believes you're a bad lot," he said. "There's nothing anyone would like better than to see you make good. There's been some talk about it at the school. Everyone, including your guardian, the child welfare services and the police, agrees that you are in the best place."

It was well put. As though he himself had no part in it, but had merely been given the task of delivering the message.

"Personally, I can well understand you," he said, "but after what has happened, I think it's highly unlikely that anyone else at the school could be persuaded to recommend your getting out of here."

I waited until night-time, there was really no place where you could be alone in the daytime. You slept three to a room; when the other two were asleep I slipped out to the toilet.

The toilets were the same as at Crusty House, there was a radiator and the light was left on all night. You could not lock the door, but everything was quiet.

I slit the spine of the *Folk High School Song Book*; I had taken a new Stanley knife-blade from the workshop, even with that it was a slow job, you could feel how the binding had been made to last as long as ten or twenty years. In the front the previous owners had written their names and the years, the first was from 1960. Tucked in next to the pages printed with the songs were the papers

242

I had taken, long ago, from Biehl's locked drawer. Still glued in and intact.

The following night I wrote to my guardian. It took half the night. I wrote in detail about how I needed to get out, just for a few hours one afternoon, to see where August had been buried, would that be possible?

I received no reply. When a week had gone by, I rang her office, the minute you heard her voice you could tell that it was out of the question.

"He's in an unmarked grave in Bispebjerg cemetery," she said. "It was the family's decision. There's nothing to see."

"I still need to see it," I said.

The officer looked at me. Leave of absence was very rarely granted, and then only with the consent of the guardian and the Department of Health and Welfare and if accompanied by an officer.

"You just don't seem to understand your situation," she said. "Not for six months, at least."

The next day I sent her another letter. I wrote asking her if she would take three photocopies of the enclosed sheets, in which case I would be forever in her debt, and would she be so kind as to send it to me in a Children's Panel envelope?

Her letter arrived two days later. Maybe she had wanted to make up for not being able to arrange leave of absence for me, I think she had. In a small way she had wanted to ask for forgiveness.

Usually, all private mail was opened and checked for drugs before being handed over, but because she had sent an official envelope I received it unopened.

The next evening I left the home for a short while.

It was Friday, there was a dance, with a band. They had invited Ravnsborg assessment centre for young girls. Fifteen girls turned up, and about twenty female staff and assistants. It was the first time in the history of the home that girls had been admitted, it was part of the new educational policy of the time.

All their attention was focused on the assembly hall where the band was playing, and on checking whether anyone was drinking or breaking any other rules. It had not entered their heads that anyone would try, right now, to run away from the school.

The gate was manned, but there was no problem. Normally the fence was lit up, but they had used the searchlights to light the stage, everything was in darkness, I had the time I needed.

There were gates in both the outer and the inner fences, both fitted with standard padlocks, and reinforced with chains. To make absolutely certain, I had borrowed a small drill from the workshop, I drilled through them.

I walked from the home to the Kalundborg motorway and hitched. Taking the bus would have entailed too great a risk, the home had an arrangement with West Zealand Transport Company, who reported anyone looking like an inmate who got on near Ravnsborg.

I was given two good lifts and a bad one. When he put his hand on me I just said: "I'll stick my finger down my throat and throw up in your car." That made him keep his distance, it usually does. I was dropped off on Ålekistevej, from there I walked the rest of the way along the side of Damhus Lake.

It was not cold – mild, more like. It had stayed light for a long time and even though it was now dark the light had not disappeared, but lay sort of enfolded in the night. That is what I thought. I suppose there have always been light summer nights in your life, but there comes a time when, for the first time, you tell yourself that this is so. For me it came that night.

The gate to the grounds was locked, but not the little door. I came up past the storehouse, it had been rebuilt and freshly painted, and the trees closest to it were still charred – apart from that there was nothing to be seen.

All the lights in the annexe were out, including the one in Flakke-dam's room and that of the new superintendent. In the main building a solitary light burned, right at the top, in Biehl's flat.

There was a new lock on the door under the archway, I tried using my sheet-metal copy, it did not fit, so I drilled through the lock, at the join of the tumbler and the cylinder casing; it took less than five minutes. On the way up the stairs I tried a few of the doors on to the corridors, the entire lock system had been replaced.

Clearly this was because of what had happened with us. They had replaced them in order, somehow, to make it easier to forget us and make a fresh start.

I ascended to the fifth floor and let myself into the corridor with the drill, and from there into the assembly hall. I came past Delling, who unlocks the gates of morning, and from there through the little door that led to Biehl's office, the one through which he entered in the mornings and ascended the podium.

The room was as I remembered. But there was a key in the wooden chest now. I felt inside, it was empty. Now it was only for show, the papers had been moved to a safer place. A wise move, I had never understood why they had been kept in such an exposed position.

I sat down at his desk. Not in his chair, but in the one kept for adult visitors, it had arms and was upholstered. I had carried the papers in my shoe, between the insole and the sole, I took them out and placed them on the desk. There was enough light from outside to read by. From the moon and the stars and the night-enfolded gleam of daylight.

There were two A4 sheets, closely written and three-quarters covered, in black ink. It was Biehl's handwriting, he always wrote with a fountain pen and black ink.

The paper was made exclusively from rags.

There was no way of telling this – it felt like ordinary paper, but thicker – it was something we had been told. Biehl had said that this was one of the signs of the current state of decay, that the quality of paper grew steadily poorer. For especially important documents – diplomas, end-of-the-year gradings, recommendations and reports on pupils and teachers, the school used rag paper with a watermark, both for the originals and for the copies. The Ministry of Education required that these be kept on file, along with examination returns, for at least ten years after the person concerned had left the school. Rag paper, Biehl had said, does not fade.

When you held the sheet up towards the window you could see the watermark – Odin's ravens, Hugin and Munin.

Across the ravens flowed the black lines of writing – figures, letters and symbols. On all the sheets there was not one single word in full. The figures were obviously dates. Against each date there were several letters and a symbol, a diagonal stroke or a cross or, now and then, a circle. The first date was 4 August 1970.

At another time in your life you would not have grasped the significance of this list, you would have looked at it and not made head nor tail of it, and then forgotten it. It obviously had something to do with the past two school years, the first date was less than a week after the first day of school last year. Apart from that it would have held no meaning. And yet I had understood it the moment I saw it, that first time, under the blank sheets of school rag paper, while August sat on a chair, half asleep, when he was still alive.

It was because it came into my hands at a time when I was constantly thinking about time. When I remembered all the dates that I had been late, or had handed in work late, and when I had seen Katarina in the playground and when August came to the school and started attracting the wrong sort of attention.

All of this I had tried to remember, because that is what you do when time threatens to slip away from you. You try to remember everything so as to hold on to it. In desperation many dates had entered my head and some of them had stuck. On Biehl's sheet of paper I saw my own initials. I recognised them because they were set against the two dates when I had been summoned to his office. I saw August's and Katarina's initials too, and the times when they had been to the office – Katarina's twice, the two times she had had to make use of in order to understand Biehl and to see where the switchboard sat and work out where the clock was.

Against her and August's and my name, every time, there was a diagonal stroke, apart from in one place, 9 September, where there was a cross against me. That had been the first and only time that Biehl had hit me, at that point I had been registered as having been late six times in less than twenty school days.

After each set of initials he had noted which class the pupil was in, I found CS for Carsten Sutton, there were a lot of entries for him, it looked like a record. Every time, against his name, there was a cross. You knew that he had never been summoned to the office for less than a clout round the ear.

He had been expelled at the beginning of November 1970, for the incident with the cellulose thinner and what followed. The day before, I had seen him coming from Biehl's office, it was the first

246

time I had seen him cry, you would not have thought him capable of it. Biehl had a little fibreglass pointer which he brought along whenever he needed to point out something on the maps of the world. It had a cork handle like a fishing rod, he preferred this to the stiff wooden pointers provided in the classrooms, someone said he had used the fibreglass pointer on Sutton.

That day, against Sutton's initials, CS, and 2nd sec. for the class he was in, there was a circle.

When I came to the school, there was talk about the fact that a recommendation had been received from the Ministry of Education, saying that sex education ought to be taught at the school. Biehl had come right out and said that the teachers had been unanimous in deciding not to comply with this recommendation. Instead it would be up to the individual teacher to bring up the subject whenever it was judged to fit naturally into a lesson.

Which meant that it was never brought up directly. Although hints were given – in Biehl's Greek mythology classes when he told us about Zeus and those he had raped, and especially in Fredhøj's classes when he read, for example, about the wife-killer. And it was Fredhøj who told us about the masturbation marks in Hans Christian Andersen's diaries.

Secret symbols. Every time Hans Christian Andersen had jerked off, he had put a mark in his diary.

A bit like the marks Madvig had made.

Stuus, the school's Latin teacher, was a university man, like Biehl, and therefore almost overqualified. It was a measure of the school's calibre that it had a teacher like him. He only took the leaving-certificate classes – for French, too – but now and again you had him as a relief teacher. He never remembered a single pupil's name, or what sort of class he was in. Even so you sensed that if you left him alone he would do you no harm.

He had told us about Madvig. Madvig was a nineteenth-century Danish philologist and educational reformer. His works on Greek and Latin had sent the name of Denmark flying out across the world. Stuus said that Madvig had never been to Greece and only once to Italy, it was as though it was not so much the country or its people that had interested him as the extinct language. He had had a big Greek dictionary, it was still around, in it he had set a blue dot alongside a word the first time he looked it up, and a red dot if he had to look it up a second time. In the whole dictionary there were only a very few red dots.

Hans Christian Andersen and Madvig, both had kept a discreet account. Then immediately you understand, but still it is hard to say exactly what they were recording. It must have been something to do with shame and love and time and control and memory. And perhaps a certain pleasure in being able to document your weakness, your illness. A secret delight over the solitary craving, the solitary forgetfulness and recall.

Biehl's list was a secret account of which pupils he had punished. Specifying date and punishment. There were three possibilities, the paper had recorded three forms. The verbal reprimand. The standard blow. And something exceptional. Beating. A circle.

When an explanation had been demanded of Biehl – because Jes Jessen's right ear had hurt and his doctor had said that it looked as though it was a result of the outer ear having been molested, and why had they waited six weeks before taking him to the casualty department? – then he had explained that it had been a spontaneous act. Boxing a pupil's ears was something that happened suddenly, it was uncalculated. Granted, he had said, this was perhaps not the best solution, but afterwards the air was cleared, and if you asked the children they would tell you that they preferred this to more long-term measures.

Even so, he had kept an account. In his heart of hearts he had felt a need to create an overall picture for himself, to have visible proof of how time and punishment were bound up with his own life. Perhaps to prevent himself from hitting out too often, or perhaps to have a better idea of which pupils had repeatedly merited it, or perhaps just out of a need to keep track of time, or perhaps out of a certain pleasure – or perhaps all of these reasons at one and the same time.

Hans Christian Andersen's marks, Madvig's dots, Biehl's symbols. Something to do with time, improvement, control, memory. And pleasure.

As though one part of their nature were attempting to repress another. To keep it under some sort of surveillance.

They have run a sort of risk with their signs, especially Biehl. As though one part of him has longed for exposure.

As though this exposure has been part of the plan.

In Danish Primary and Lower-Secondary Schools there is a ban on striking pupils, there was a ban on it back then, there had been a ban on it since the Ministry of Education circular on disciplinary measures in schools of 14 June 1967, which replaced the physical contact circular of 1929 (augmented 1945). This had affirmed that teachers should have as little physical contact with pupils as possible, so as not to be misunderstood, preferably limited to dishing out clouts on the ear.

Danish private schools were subject to standard Danish educational legislation, government grants covered more than eighty per cent of their running costs. By, nevertheless, regularly meting out physical punishment to pupils, the school and Biehl in particular had been running a risk. This he must have known. The pupils were not aware of this, nor the parents, the school was shut off from the outside world. We who attended it were the only ones who really knew what went on within its walls. And even we hovered in a certain ignorance. What happened in Biehl's office and in Fredhøj's office and in Karin Ærø's classes was not something you spoke about, that was between teacher and pupil.

Still, even though so few were aware of what was going on, they must have known that they were very close to the limit.

I raised him on the intercom.

It was a grey box, you had seen it before without really paying much attention, it was not much bigger than a telephone. It had grooves through which to speak and listen, and numbered buttons – sixty-three of them, pretty small. On the desk there was a type-written list assigning each number to a room, it looked as though there were buttons for every room in the school.

Three wires led from the instrument. One went into the plug, for the power, the second went into a box on the wall and must have been the link with the loudspeakers in all the school classrooms. The third ran across the floor and along the panelling and up along the door and through the wall. Out in the corridor it must have run up through the ceiling, diagonally across, through the wall and into Bürk's pendulum clock, from which impulses would be emitted whenever classes were to be let out or called in.

When the loudspeakers had been installed Biehl had said just the one thing – this was at Assembly – he had said that the electronic bell had a more pleasant sound.

Against number 23 the label read PRIVATE APARTMENT. I pressed it, the button stayed down, but nothing happened. At the top there were two switches, one dark and one lighter. When I pressed the light one I got through to Biehl's flat.

At first there was almost nothing, just a hiss, but I knew that I was there.

It was impossible to imagine how it must look, no one had ever been up there. What I sensed was all the space and the light. The feeling that it was a home – even now when his children were all grown up, the feeling was still there. He had three children, all three of them teachers, they had held posts here at the school. Pale and quiet as though they had not had enough light. But still his children. I listened and I was with a family.

Then china was placed on china, a cup on a saucer, his tea, quite close to my ear. Then he cleared his throat. He was alone, this I could hear. He had no idea that I was listening. That was how the intercom was designed, you could listen without being heard yourself. That was how he himself must have sat, listening in to the classes.

I pressed the dark button, and a little green light came on below the grooves.

"Excuse me," I said.

At first there was no sound. Then I could sense that he had come right up close to the microphone.

"Peter," he said.

He was brilliant. There was hardly any reaction. Ever so calmly he had bowed his head and taken the problem upon himself.

"I hope I'm not disturbing you," I said.

"Are you alone?"

I did not answer this question.

"I have a document I would like permission to present."

He appeared a moment later, he was alone, he was in his braces. The same type of grey trousers as always and a white shirt, but no jacket. He had moved his watch from the jacket down to his trousers, you could see the chain.

He remained standing in the centre of the room. I suppose it was the first time ever that he had been the one to come through the door, with someone else waiting for him.

He switched on the light, his eyes found the paper immediately, he had always known it would be this.

"Give me that," he said.

I handed him the list. He folded it and tore it in half, and folded it and tore it, and folded it and tore it, and put the pieces in his pocket.

"Did you slit open my satchel?" I said. He did not answer, that was answer enough.

I gave him the list again. "These are copies," I said, "photocopies, I've just tucked the original back into my shoe, back at home I have more copies."

He waited, very aware.

"If the Children's Panel see this," I said, "and the accompanying explanation, they'll have a word with the Ministry of Education. And they'll have a word with you, and with the school board, and the parents' council. And then they'll start to question all the pupils on that list, and they'll find out about Carsten Sutton and go back in time to Jes Jessen, and I'll be questioned too, there'll be a long, long line of confrontations, it will be disastrous. What can be done to avoid this?"

It was almost overwhelming. All his life he had worked and fought for this school – you knew this, of course, from his memoirs – and considered himself in tune with time and eternal values. At heart he had known that his intentions were good. And yet he had ended up here.

It was hard to say whose fault it was, even today I do not know, even for the department it would have been almost impossible to unravel the threads and allocate the blame.

He looked careworn. He had often talked about God. But I do not believe that he had ever, until this moment, sensed so acutely the way that a purpose and a plan greater than himself had taken hold of him.

He was confronted with what he had always said was the most detestable thing of all, concealment and doubt. To look at him was shattering. All his life he had believed that he was fighting for good. And still.

"I want to be adopted," I said. "The National Council for the Unmarried Mother and her Child will ask the school for a statement. I would be grateful if it could be no worse than is necessary."

He said not one word in reply. He turned and went, leaving me alone. I stayed there only for a moment, and sat and looked out at the heavens. Then I left, it was his office, after all. You had no right to be there.